THE EVERYTHING® KIDS' BASEBALL BOOK

12th Edition

A guide to today's stars, all-time greats, and legendary teams—with tips on playing like a pro

Joe Gergen

Adams Media

New York London Toronto Sydney New Delhi

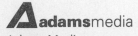

Adams Media
An Imprint of Simon & Schuster, Inc.
100 Technology Center Drive
Stoughton, Massachusetts 02072

An Everything® Series Book.

Everything® and everything.com® are registered trademarks of Simon & Schuster, Inc.

This Adams Media trade paperback edition March 2022

ADAMS MEDIA and colophon are trademarks of Simon & Schuster.

For information about special discounts for bulk purchases, please contact Simon & Schuster Special Sales at 1-866-506-1949 or business@simonandschuster.com.

The Simon & Schuster Speakers Bureau can bring authors to your live event. For more information or to book an event contact the Simon & Schuster Speakers Bureau at 1-866-248-3049 or visit our website at www.simonspeakers.com.

Interior layout by Colleen Cunningham and Alaya Howard
Illustrations by Jim Steck
Puzzles by Beth L. Blair and Jim Steck

Manufactured in the United States of America

Printed by Lakeside Book Company, Harrisonburg, VA, U.S.A.

1 2022

ISBN 978-1-5072-1806-8
ISBN 978-1-5072-1807-5 (ebook)

For Judy Dowling Wolf, a cousin
who raised two major leaguers—
pitcher Randy and umpire Jim.

Contents

Introduction

Do you remember the feeling you had when you got your first glove? The excitement of catching a ball for the very first time? How about watching your favorite player hit a walk-off home run? People around the world have been playing, watching, and arguing about baseball for 150 years...and why not? Baseball is America's pastime!

Whether you're a super fan or completely new to the sport, this book has something to offer you:

- If you're new to the game or are looking for new ways to play, check out **Chapter 1**. There you'll find all the rules of play, along with tips for developing your hitting and defensive skills.

- Learn about the origins of the game and the original stars of baseball in **Chapter 2**, with a look at the history and evolution of the sport from the 1800s to today.

- **Chapters 3 and 4** cover the National and American Leagues and the legendary players from each team. Baseball and softball players outside the major leagues are featured in **Chapter 8**.

- Today's greatest players and the Baseball Hall of Fame are the focus of **Chapter 5**.

- Do you love to keep track of player and team statistics, record holders, and league standings? You'll find all that and more in **Chapter 7**.

- **Chapter 9** is your guide to being a super fan. You'll get advice on drafting your own fantasy baseball team and creating a baseball card collection. And if you've always wanted to learn how to score a game, there's a step-by-step guide to filling out an official scorecard.

The Everything® Kids' Baseball Book, 12th Edition can be your guide to baseball past and baseball present. It's certainly fun to read straight through, but it can also be a useful reference. Are your grandparents always talking about the 1975 World Series? Read about what they saw in the list of notable Series games. Is your sister always checking the box scores in the newspaper or online? Use this book to find out what those columns of numbers mean. Do you want to become a better player? Try some of the skill-building exercises or learn a new game like Off the Wall or Punchball. And throughout the book you'll find fun puzzles and activities to keep you occupied when you can't get outside to play.

Ready to get started? Step up to the plate and...

Baseball is a great game, one that is played and enjoyed by tens of millions of people. Many of those who appreciate the game grew up playing and watching baseball. Few get good enough to be major leaguers, but everyone can learn how to play, and everyone can, with practice, become a better player. This chapter covers the fundamentals of baseball: the rules, the necessary skills, the positions of the players, and some ways to play baseball even if you don't have two teams of nine players available.

Rules of the Game

Baseball, at its heart, is a very simple game. A batter hits the ball, then tries to make it to first base (or farther!) without getting called out. Someone who gets all the way around the bases scores a run; whichever team scores the most runs during the game wins.

Teams take turns at bat. A team keeps batting until they make three outs; then they pitch to the other team until *they* make three outs. After each team has had nine turns, the game is over.

Here are the most common ways for the batter to make an out:

- **Strikeout.** A batter gets a strike if he swings and misses, or if he doesn't swing at a good pitch. Three strikes and the batter is out.
- **Flyout.** If a fielder catches a batted ball before it hits the ground, the batter is out.
- **Groundout.** If a fielder throws the ball to first base before the batter gets there, the batter is out.
- **Tagged out.** If a runner is not touching a base and is tagged with the ball, the runner is out.

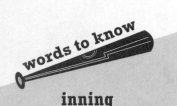

words to know

inning

A period of play in which each team has a turn at bat. A professional or college baseball game lasts for nine innings. High school and Little League games are usually shorter—five, six, or seven innings.

There's much, much more to the rules of baseball, but you learn by playing and watching the game. Even professional players are still learning about the game. That's part of what makes baseball such a wonderful sport!

Developing Your Baseball Skills

How can you develop your baseball skills? The answer is simple: play. Play a lot. Play with your friends, play in a league or two, play in the backyard with your family. The more you play, the more you'll learn about the game. You'll develop baseball instincts—you'll know what to do on the bases or in the field without even thinking about it. Your skills will get better and better. And whether or not you become a great player, you will likely develop a deep appreciation for the game of baseball that you can share with your friends and family. Many adults' most heartfelt memories are of playing and watching baseball when they were kids your age.

For professional baseball, you need two teams of nine players, each with uniforms and gloves, several brand-new baseballs, and some umpires...but all you *really* need to play a game is a few friends, an old tennis ball, and a stick for a bat.

words to know

umpire

A person who is ruling on the plays in the game. The umpire rules whether a pitch is a strike or a ball; if a ball that is hit is fair or foul; and if a batter or runner is safe or out.

Hitting

To become a good hitter, you have to hit—a lot. Of course you'll get to hit in games, but if you want to get more hitting practice, try these ideas:

- **Take a bucket of balls out to an empty field.** Have a friend pitch them all to you. Pick up all the balls and then you pitch them all to your friend.

- **Get some Wiffle balls.** Wiffle balls are plastic balls with holes in them. Since they won't go far, they are less likely to hurt someone or something. Wiffle balls are good for playing with on a small field or in the backyard.
- **Hit balls off of a tee.** You can practice hitting the ball in different directions: Try hitting ten balls to left field, ten to center field, then ten to right field.
- **Go to a batting cage.** A machine will pitch a ball to you, and you can decide how fast you want the ball to come toward you.

Hitting Practice Is the Time to Experiment

Try out different kinds of bats—heavy bats, light bats, long bats, short bats, wooden bats, and metal bats. You don't necessarily have to buy yourself a brand-new bat to try it out. Ask to borrow a bat from a friend, or buy a cheap used bat at a secondhand store.

Then try different ways to stand. Mimic your favorite player's stance. Try out some of the advice a coach or a friend gave you. Find out what feels the most comfortable. As long as you can see the ball well, and you can keep your eye on the ball when you make contact, then your stance is fine. You may fine-tune it someday, but for now, go with what feels the best.

Most importantly, work on making contact with the ball. Don't worry about how hard you hit it—don't swing hard to hit home runs—just practice *hitting* the ball with every swing. After all this hitting practice, you'll find your hitting in games to be more consistent. Your body will know exactly what to do. You'll end up getting on base a lot. Eventually, without even trying, you'll start hitting the ball harder.

fun fact

What Is a Slump?

A slump is when a hitter stops getting hits for a while. Slumps happen to all hitters, even the best. Usually a slump lasts for only a few games, but sometimes it will go on for weeks. Hitters will try everything from extra batting practice to good luck charms to get out of a slump. When you get in a slump, just relax and try not to get too frustrated—all slumps have to end sometime.

Defense

The team that isn't batting is called the defense. Their job is to field the ball and put the batters out. The nine players on defense play the different positions described in the following list. Each position requires slightly different skills, though all defensive players must be able to throw well.

- **Infielders.** Those who play first base, second base, third base, and shortstop are called infielders. Infielders play close to the batter and to the bases. They field ground balls and try to throw the batter out. When a ball is hit into the outfield, the infielders receive the ball from the outfielders and try to tag out runners.
- **Outfielders.** The right fielder, left fielder, and center fielder are the outfielders. They play far away from the batter and the bases. Their main job is to catch fly balls and to throw the ball back to the infielders.
- **Catcher.** The catcher crouches behind home plate to catch any pitches that the batter doesn't hit. If a runner tries to steal a base, the catcher throws the ball to try to get the runner out.
- **Pitcher.** The pitcher starts all the action on the field by throwing every pitch to the batter. Pitchers also have to field ground balls and help out the infielders.

The best way to improve your baseball skills is to play in lots of games. A fielder needs to develop a "baseball sense" in addition to physical skills. This means not just being able to field and throw the ball but also knowing *where* to throw the ball and where to be on the field. When you're in the field, think to yourself before every pitch: If the ball comes to me, what do I do with it? If the ball doesn't come to me, where am I supposed to go? By answering these questions

⭐ Look for Signs

Some people hold up signs in the stands, but in baseball there are other signs. The catcher puts down fingers to give the pitcher a sign as to what pitch to throw. There are also signs relayed from the coach at third base to the batter. Coaches are usually busy touching their cap, tugging on their ear, and doing all sorts of movements. They are signaling the batter to take a pitch, swing away, bunt, or perhaps hit and run. They are also often signaling runners on base. Next time you're at a game, watch the third-base coach for a minute and see what he's up to. If you're playing, always check what the sign from the coach is before the pitcher pitches. ⭐

before every pitch in every game you play, you will build up good baseball instincts that you may not even be aware of. You'll find yourself making great plays simply because you knew what to do before the batter even hit the ball.

Throwing

The most important defensive skill, regardless of position, is throwing. Everyone on the field needs to be able to throw accurately over short and long distances.

How do you get good at throwing? Practice. Find a friend, grab your gloves, and play catch. Don't throw as hard or as fast as you can; just stand at a comfortable distance and practice throwing the ball right to your friend. For example, see how many throws you can make to each other without dropping the ball. Once you can make thirty or forty throws in a row, each of you take a big step back and try again from the longer distance.

If you want to practice throwing by yourself, find a heavy, solid wall, like the backboard at a tennis or handball court. Use chalk to lightly mark a square about chest high. Using a tennis ball, try to hit the wall inside the square. You can design a game—call a "strike" if the ball hits inside the square, and call a "ball" if the ball hits on the line or outside the square. Try to earn a strikeout by throwing three strikes before you throw four balls. Once strikeouts become easy, take a step back and try again, or redraw a smaller square.

Fielding Ground Balls

When the batter hits a ground ball, the infielders try to pick up the ball, then throw to first base quickly to put the batter out. When you are developing your skill at fielding ground balls, don't worry about making the throw to first base. Start by making sure you can catch the ball every time.

Playing with Ghosts?

You can play baseball with as few as two or three players per team. But what do you do if a three-player team loads the bases so that the next batter is standing on third base? You put a "ghost runner" on third. The other runners run the bases as normal, but everyone pretends that the ghost runner is running too. You should make rules ahead of time about how to put a ghost runner out!

Shuffle your feet to get your body in front of the ball; watch the ball all the way until it is inside your glove. Try to be in such a good position that anytime the ball takes a funny hop, it hits you in the leg or in the chest and stops nearby. That way you'll still be able to pick up the ball quickly.

The way to get good at fielding grounders is (surprise!) to practice. Set up some bases with a couple of friends. Put one person at bat, one person at first base, and one person at shortstop. Have the batter hit ground balls toward the shortstop, who should field them and throw to first base. Keep this up until the shortstop successfully fields five or ten balls in a row, then rotate who gets to play shortstop. Two friends can also roll grounders to each other. You can even practice grounders by throwing a tennis ball against a wall and fielding the rebound.

Catching Fly Balls

Outfielders especially have to practice fielding fly balls. The hardest part of catching flies is figuring out where the ball is headed. Once you know where the ball is going to land, run to that spot, turn toward the ball with your glove above your head, and catch the ball in front of you.

Try not to have to catch a ball while you're still running—this makes it harder to judge where the ball is, so it's more likely you'll drop it. Also, if you're running, it will be harder to make the throw back to the infield. Of course, sometimes a ball is hit so far away from you that the only way to catch it is to keep running as hard as you can the whole way. But if you can manage to stop before you catch the ball, do it.

Fly ball practice is best done with a real batter, not just with someone throwing the ball in the air. Try to get friends to hit fly balls to you, especially if you have some friends

Pitchers: Work Quickly

The best pitchers take their position on the pitching rubber without wasting time between pitches. The mechanics of a pitch itself should never be rushed—the windup and delivery should be the same every time. But walking around the mound, thinking for a long time, or paying too much attention to a base runner hurts a pitcher's performance. You don't want to give the batter time to think about your next pitch; you want your fielders alert and ready, not kicking dirt out of boredom while waiting for action.

Even Major Leaguers Practice

One time, the great San Diego hitter Tony Gwynn didn't get a hit in a game that lasted until almost midnight. According to baseball lore, on his way home, Gwynn stopped by his old high school, where he had a key to the batting cage. He practiced hitting in the cage for about an hour before he went to bed.

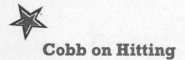

fun fact

Little League Facts

Little League baseball began in 1939 in Williamsport, Pennsylvania, where the Little League World Series is still played today. Little League baseball is popular with boys and girls of all ages, from all over the world. Teams usually have between twelve and twenty players on them, and everyone on a team should get a chance to play.

Cobb on Hitting

Ty Cobb was one of the best hitters ever. He recommended that hitters not hold the bat all the way at the bottom. He suggested holding the hands an inch from the knob and keeping the hands an inch apart from each other for better balance and bat control. Not everyone should hit this way, but Ty Cobb had a career .366 batting average and made the Hall of Fame, so his advice might work!

who are good batters. High school kids or adults can give the best fly ball practice, because they might have better bat control to hit a lot of good fly balls.

Pitching

In the major leagues, pitchers are specialists—that is, their job is only to pitch, and they rarely work on any other skills or play any other positions. Major league pitchers spend their practice time building arm and leg strength, practicing different types of pitches, and resting their arms.

When younger people play baseball, however, the pitcher is just a good player who can throw the ball accurately. Pitchers who aren't pitching usually play elsewhere in the field. It is far, far more important for a pitcher to be able to hit a target than for a pitcher to throw hard or to throw different pitches.

Professional pitchers throw 80, 90, or even 100 miles per hour; they throw curve balls, knuckle balls, sliders, and fork balls. But they are *professionals*. They are pitching to the best hitters in the world, so they must take every advantage they can find.

The best youth league and even high school pitchers don't necessarily throw hard or curvy stuff. They throw a fastball consistently to the catcher's glove every time whether the catcher asks for a pitch inside or outside, high or low.

What kind of pitch can you throw besides a fastball? Try a changeup. You normally grip a fastball with your thumb and your first two fingers. Instead, try holding the ball all the way back in your palm, but use the same motion as you do for a fastball. You should find that this pitch goes just a bit slower; that's a changeup. Changeups are hard to hit because they throw off the batter's timing—the batter will

Why do hitters like night baseball?

Connect the dots to find the answer to the above riddle.

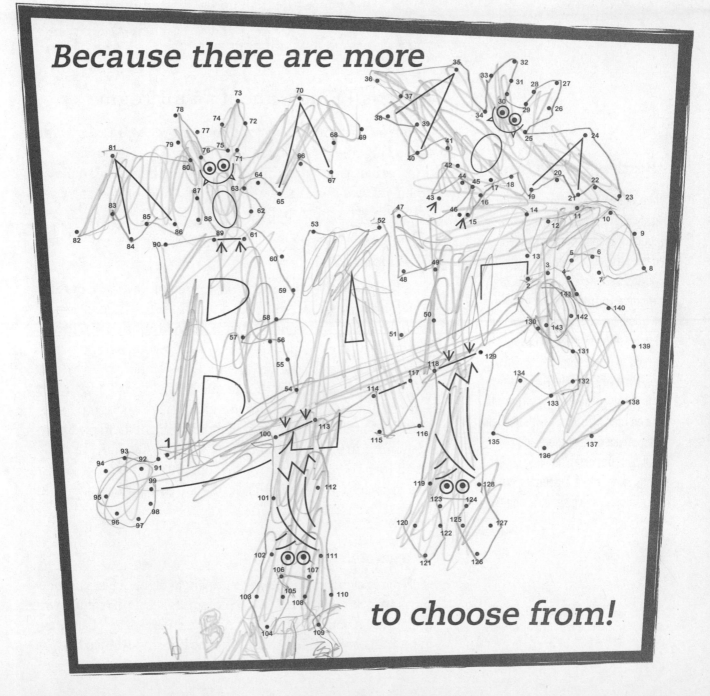

Because there are more

to choose from!

be starting to swing just before the ball gets to the plate. If you can throw just a fastball and a changeup, and if you can throw them right to the catcher's glove on every pitch, then you will be an outstanding young pitcher.

Baseball Fun Without a Full Team

If you're short on players or equipment but you really want to play a game of baseball, don't panic! There are a few alternatives that are similar to baseball that you can play when you only have a few friends available or you can't get your hands on a bat, ball, or glove.

Punchball

This game uses the same basic idea of baseball, but if you don't have gloves, bats, or a field handy, you can use a tennis ball, or even a heavy wad of taped-up paper. Throw the ball up above your head, then swing your extended arm like a bat and "punch" the ball. Position as many fielders as you have at bases and in the outfield. You don't need a pitcher or a catcher, and if you don't have enough people to fill the other positions, you can shrink the field and play with only three bases and two outfielders (it's hard to punch a ball into the outfield, anyway). Punchball is a good alternative to baseball or softball if you're looking for a baseball-like game to play with friends.

Two-Ball

This is a good baseball game for six to eight players. Divide the players into teams of two. Each pair takes a turn at bat while everyone else plays in the field. A pitcher pitches to a batter as in normal baseball. The batter hits the ball and runs to first, but

Batting Cage Game

When you go to a batting cage, you usually get ten swings for a certain amount of money. You and a friend can have a friendly game of batting cage baseball. Here's how it works: Every time you make contact, you get 1 point, even if you hit a foul ball. Every time you hit the ball beyond the pitching machine, you get 2 points. Every time you miss the ball, you lose 1 point. This game helps you concentrate on making contact with the ball. As you make contact more and more, you'll feel comfortable taking bigger swings to get more 2-pointers, but you may also miss and lose some points.

Curve Ball

The curve ball is one of the trickiest pitches to hit.
See if you can score by running a line of color through each of the
curvy baseball terms in the following list! Instead of reading in a straight
line, each word has one bend in it. Words can go in any direction.

HINT: One word has been done for you.

ASTROTURF

BLEACHERS

DUGOUT

HOME RUN

HOT DOG

POP FLY

SCOREBOARD

SHORTSTOP

STADIUM

WORLD SERIES

```
F L Y L E B O A R D T O
U P O R R L E R N S J P
G R O M F E S E I R E S
A C U P D A T S C T M D
S S T G I C O S H I R L
T K R U U H H N D S N R
R B O E M O R E P U T O
I O U S R H O T R S G W
H O T T S T O P E S O O
O M D U S H O T M T U B
T D O L R K O T O A T L
R O G D B F E O H D M A
```

Catching with Style?

You might have seen a major leaguer make what looks like a cool catch on an easy play. For example, outfielder Dave Parker of the Pirates and Reds used to flip his glove down for a "snap catch." Although he was a Hall of Fame leadoff hitter and base stealer, Rickey Henderson yanked his glove sideways when he caught fly balls. Any coach will tell you that making a fancy catch in a game is a bad idea— you could drop the ball!

fun fact

Other "Little" Leagues

Even if you're not ready for official Little League ball, you might have other options. In tee-ball, there's no pitcher—the batter just hits the ball off of a tee. Other leagues allow coaches to pitch to the players or limit each inning to nine batters. Ask around to find out what kinds of leagues for young players are available in your community.

the batter is out if any fielder can touch the ball before the batter reaches first base. Then the batter's partner bats.

The batting pair doesn't run the bases: Base runners are ghost runners who advance whenever the batter gets a hit. After the batters make three outs, they go into the field, and the next pair comes in to bat. This is a fun but exhausting game. On offense, it will help you develop your ability to hit the ball where you want it to go; defenders will develop their throwing range. Oh, and playing this game will help make sure you're in shape!

Off the Wall

This is a fun game you can play with two people, a ball, a glove, and a wall. You don't even need a glove if you're using a softer ball like a tennis ball.

Find a wall without windows where it's okay to throw a ball. You can use a vacant racquetball court, one wall of a gymnasium, or even the side of a barn. Next to the wall, mark off a territory to designate what is fair and what is foul. Use an area big enough that you can run from one end to the other in not too many steps. (Experiment to get the size right.)

To play, one player throws the ball high off the wall and the other person has to catch it. If the catcher catches the ball without it bouncing on the ground, he or she gets an "out." If the catcher drops it, the person throwing the ball has a runner on first base. If the ball bounces once before being caught, it's a single; twice, it's a double; three times, it's a triple; and four times, it's a home run. Always remember where your runners are, and keep track of how many runs you each score. Don't choose a space too big, or you'll never be able to cover the ground. Also, make a rule against throwing the ball so close to the wall that the only way to catch it is by crashing into the wall. Off the Wall is a good way to practice covering ground in the outfield and catching fly balls.

Chapter 2
The History of Baseball

fun fact

Vintage Base Ball

You can still watch Base Ball (as it was called in the mid-1800s) in its vintage form. There are more than three hundred clubs in the Vintage Base Ball Association, whose players dress in authentic 1800s uniforms and play games by 1800s rules. Players don't wear gloves or any protective equipment, like catcher's masks or batting helmets. Team names come from local teams that once existed, including the Detroit Early Risers, the Boston Beaneaters, and the Cincinnati Red Stockings.

There are thirty major league teams today, and many more minor league teams with players hoping to make it to the big leagues. There are thousands of college teams, high school teams, and Little League teams all playing baseball. But where did it all begin? How did the major leagues get started? This chapter will answer all your questions!

The Earliest Games

Baseball has been played for well over 150 years. The game became well known throughout the United States during and after the Civil War in the 1860s. Before then, pitchers threw underhand, no one had gloves, the ball was softer than what we know as a baseball today, and the bases were forty-two paces (probably about 120 feet) from each other—but it was baseball. The idea was to hit the ball, get from base to base safely, and score runs before getting three outs in your team's turn at bat.

Amateur teams were formed, and they played until the first team scored 21 runs, which at that time took only a few innings. In 1857, the idea of playing a nine-inning game was introduced, the bases were placed 90 feet apart, and more rules were changed.

The First Professional Teams

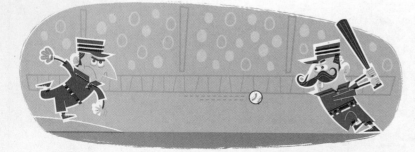

As far back as the 1860s there were barnstorming teams, which were teams that went from city to city playing each other. The first of these teams to be made up entirely of paid players was the Cincinnati Red Stockings of 1869. That first professional team's record was 57-0.

In 1871, the National Association of Professional Base Ball Players was formed with nine teams. The Philadelphia Athletics were the first champions, winning twenty-one games and losing only seven. By 1875, too much gambling caused people to lose interest in this league, but not in baseball. In 1876, the National League was formed. Many players from the original association became part of this new league, including Cap Anson, who was considered one of the game's first star players.

Through the 1880s and 1890s, several other leagues, including the American Association, the Players League, and a minor league called the Western League, began. All except the Western League failed.

Baseball Through the Decades

The modern era of baseball is said to have begun in 1900. Here is a look at what happened in baseball history in each of the decades of the 1900s and in the current century.

1900–1909

World Championships: Cubs (2), Boston Americans, New York Giants, White Sox, Pirates

Most Famous Players: Honus Wagner, Nap Lajoie, Ty Cobb, Cy Young, Christy Mathewson

In 1901, the Western League turned into the American League and started taking players from the National League. National League team owners were none too happy about this. The unfriendliness between the two leagues lasted for 2 years, until they finally united in 1903 and came up with the idea of a World Series between the two leagues.

The first decade of the 1900s featured a great Chicago Cubs team that won 116 games and lost only thirty-six in

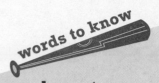

words to know

home team

The team that is playing at its own field. The home team bats second in each inning, so they always have the last chance to score runs in the game.

fun fact

The Curse of the Bambino

Between 1903 and 1918, the Boston Red Sox won the World Series five times. Following the 1919 season, the Red Sox traded Babe Ruth ("the Bambino") to the New York Yankees. After the trade, the Red Sox didn't win another World Series for 86 years. They lost in the deciding game of the playoffs or World Series on six occasions. This misfortune is called the Curse of the Bambino.

1906. They played in three World Series and won two of them. The Cubs featured an incredible infield combination that included Joe Tinker at shortstop, Johnny Evers at second base, and Frank Chance at first base.

Nap Lajoie was the American League's first batting champion, with an incredible .421 batting average. That average has been topped only once ever since, by Rogers Hornsby of the St. Louis Cardinals at .424 in 1924. Ty Cobb and Honus Wagner were great hitters and had tremendous speed, stealing plenty of bases. Pitching was very different then: There were only five or six pitchers on a team, and starters pitched more often and for more innings than they do today. Hitters hit plenty of singles, doubles, and even triples, but home runs were not common, and league leaders did not top 16 homers through 1910.

1910–1919

World Championships: Red Sox (4), Philadelphia A's (3), Boston Braves, White Sox, Reds

Most Famous Players: Ty Cobb, Tris Speaker, Gavvy Cravath, Walter Johnson, Joe Jackson

The United States was immersed in the First World War during the latter part of this decade. Yet baseball continued uninterrupted. The major leagues were challenged by a new league called the Federal League, which spent a couple of years taking players away from the American and National Leagues. Finally the major leagues were able to reach an agreement with this new league, which was dissolved. John McGraw, one of baseball's all-time great managers, led the NL's New York Giants to four World Series but no championships. In the American League, the Philadelphia Athletics, led by their great manager Connie Mack, and the Boston Red Sox were the toughest teams.

fun fact

The Box Score

In the 1850s, New York newspaper writer Henry Chadwick invented a clever way of summarizing the results of a baseball game. His invention, the box score, lists the game's players and what they did in their at bats or on the pitching mound. The box scores you read today are quite similar to the ones Chadwick put together. You can learn how to read a box score in Chapter 7.

Walter Johnson won twenty or more games every year in this decade. He was truly a great pitcher. But pitching was certainly easier back in this "dead-ball era." Until about 1920, the ball was much squishier than the baseballs we play with today, and the same ball was usually used for the entire game. Gavvy Cravath of the Philadelphia Phillies led the National League in home runs six times—but he never hit more than 24 homers in a season.

1920–1929

World Championships: Yankees (3), New York Giants (2), Cleveland Indians, Washington Senators, Pirates, Cardinals, Philadelphia A's

Most Famous Players: Rogers Hornsby, Babe Ruth, Lou Gehrig, Lefty Grove, Grover Alexander

After World War I, the country entered a period called the Roaring Twenties, filled with plenty of singing, dancing, and great baseball. The Yankees began their 40-year domination of the major leagues, during which they won twenty-nine American League pennants and twenty World Championships.

The dead-ball era was over in the 1920s. Though many sluggers emerged, it was Babe Ruth who captured the imagination of the fans. His record of 60 homers in 1927 stood for 34 years; his 714 career home runs were the most ever until 1974. "The Babe" was a big hero everywhere he went, and he was the first player to make as much as $50,000, which in those days was a very high salary—equivalent to at least half a million dollars in today's money. Whether it was because of all the home runs or not, baseball reached enormous popularity in the 1920s. In 1928, sixty-one thousand people came to Yankee Stadium to watch the Yankees defeat the Cardinals in Game 1 of the World Series; nearly forty thousand attended Game 3 in

words to know

World Series

The annual championship series of MLB, which has been played between the National League (NL) and the American League (AL) each fall since 1903, with two exceptions. In 1904, the New York Giants refused to play the AL champion Boston Americans because they considered the AL to be the "minor" league. And in 1994 the series was canceled due to the players' strike.

fun fact

Black Sox

In 1919, the Chicago White Sox earned the name "Black Sox." Eight players on the team were accused of being paid by gamblers to intentionally lose the World Series to the Reds. The first commissioner of baseball banned the eight players from the game forever. One of those players, Shoeless Joe Jackson, was one of baseball's all-time greatest hitters, but because he was kicked out of baseball, Jackson is not eligible for election to the Hall of Fame.

fun fact

Who Says Baseball Is a Slow Game?

World Series games in the first decade of the 1900s usually took about an hour and a half. That's amazing, considering that even regular season games today usually take 3 hours to play.

the much smaller city of St. Louis. Baseball cemented its title as the national pastime.

1930–1939

World Championships: Yankees (5), Cardinals (2), Philadelphia A's, New York Giants, Tigers

Most Famous Players: Lefty Grove, Lou Gehrig, Johnny Mize, Jimmie Foxx, Hack Wilson, Dizzy Dean, Hank Greenberg

The Great Depression made the 1930s difficult for many Americans. Many people were out of work and money was scarce. Baseball was an escape from the tough times.

Stealing Bases

These teams are some of the first baseball teams in this country! Some are still around, while some have moved to different cities and changed their names. See if you can finish the teams' names by adding the missing letters

B-A-S-E-S.

BALTIMORE ORIOL_ _ _
_O_TON R_D _OX
N_W YORK M_T_
_ROOKLYN DODG_R_
LO_ _ _NG _LE_ _NG _L_
_TL_NT_ _ _R_VE_

Jimmie Foxx of the Philadelphia A's came close to Ruth's home run record, hitting 58 homers in one season. The Cubs' Hack Wilson set a one-season record that still holds today, driving in 191 runs. Babe Ruth played his last game for the Yankees in 1934, and then played a few with the Braves in 1935 before retiring. Ruth's teammate Lou Gehrig continued to play alongside a new teammate who appeared in 1936, another baseball legend named Joe DiMaggio. Gehrig retired because of a serious illness in 1937 after playing in 2,130 consecutive games, a record that many thought would never be broken.

Another lasting change to the game took place in 1935 in Cincinnati when the first night game was played. The idea caught on fast, and pretty soon many night games appeared on the schedule—except at Wrigley Field in Chicago, where night games were not played until 1988.

1940–1949

World Championships: Yankees (4), Cardinals (3), Reds, Tigers, Cleveland Indians

Most Famous Players: Warren Spahn, Johnny Sain, Ted Williams, Joe DiMaggio, Bob Feller

World War II was the country's main focus in the first half of the 1940s, and many ballplayers left their teams to serve in the United States military. Young players and veterans who were too old for the military made up most of the teams. Since many of the men were in the army, women's baseball teams emerged, attracting a lot of attention as they played in their own league. The movie *A League of Their Own*

fun fact

Murderers' Row

The greatest lineup in baseball history is thought to be the 1927 lineup of the New York Yankees, nicknamed "Murderers' Row." Here are the season stats of some of their best players. As you look at these, remember that in 1927 only five players hit more than 20 home runs and that 100 RBIs has always been considered to be a very good season. These guys were incredible!

Position	Name	AVG	HR	RBI
1B	Lou Gehrig	.373	47	175
2B/3B/SS	Tony Lazzeri	.309	18	102
LF	Bob Meusel	.337	8	103
CF	Earle Combs	.356	6	64
RF	Babe Ruth	.356	60	164

Uniform Numbers

The Yankees were the first team to wear numbers on their uniforms in the 1920s. They started out by assigning numbers based on the batting order: Babe Ruth always hit third, so he was number 3; Lou Gehrig always hit fourth, so he was number 4; and so on. Today the number on a player's uniform is only used to identify the player and has nothing to do with where the player bats.

fun fact

Retired Numbers

A team will sometimes retire the number of a famous player. This means that no one else on that team will wear that number again. When the Yankees retired the number 2 of Derek Jeter, it became the twenty-first number retired by the team. But he was the twenty-second player so honored—catchers Bill Dickey and Yogi Berra both wore the number 8 during their Hall of Fame careers.

Travel by Train

Today, most teams get from one city to another in a few hours by private jet. But through much of baseball's history, teams took trains on their road trips. That's the main reason why there were no major league teams out west or in the South—a trip just from New York to Chicago meant sitting (and sleeping) on the train for an entire day.

is based on this 1940s women's baseball league (see Chapter 8 for more on women in baseball).

Even though most young American men were off to war, baseball remained an important part of their lives. Soldiers were proud of their hometown teams, and they kept track of events in the major leagues as best they could. The infantrymen even used baseball questions to distinguish friend from foe. They say that General Omar Bradley once nearly failed to convince a lookout that he was an American soldier because he didn't know that the Brooklyn Dodgers played in the National League.

Most soldiers returned from the war in 1945 and 1946, and the best athletes went into (or back into) major league baseball. Ted Williams, Joe DiMaggio, and Bob Feller were among the most well-known baseball and military heroes of the day. Williams in particular had already established himself as a great hitter, batting .406 in 1941. No one has batted over .400 since then. Though he took 3 years off from baseball, Williams returned to the game in 1946 and batted over .300 every year until 1959.

Winning World War II required a full effort from all segments of American society. Afterward, many thought it ridiculous that Black men were allowed to risk their lives in battle but were not allowed to play major league baseball (among other things). Many great players, including Jackie Robinson, Cool Papa Bell, Josh Gibson, and Satchel Paige, played in the Negro Leagues. There were great players in these leagues, a number of whom would have been big stars in the major leagues if only the team owners would have let them play. In 1947, well before the civil rights movement of the 1960s, Brooklyn Dodgers general manager Branch Rickey promoted Jackie Robinson to the majors, thus breaking the "color barrier" and paving the way for the thorough integration of professional baseball over the next decades.

The Negro Leagues

The National League was formed in 1876, and in the early years of baseball people of any race could play. In fact, Moses Fleetwood Walker joined the Toledo ball club in 1884 as the first Black professional ballplayer, and others followed. But these players were treated badly by fans, opposing players, and their own teammates. Besides calling them names, white pitchers would often throw knockdown pitches at them. Little by little, there were fewer and fewer Black players in baseball. There was no written rule, but owners no longer signed Black players. Such informal—yet real—discrimination was typical in most parts of American society for a large part of the twentieth century.

Since it was becoming impossible to get into the major leagues, Black players (referred to in those days as Negroes) began forming their own teams in the 1890s. By the early 1900s, these teams were playing independently all over the eastern United States in cities like New York and Philadelphia. These teams often played exhibition games against major-league teams, and they did well. It was obvious that many of the players on these teams had the talent to play in the major leagues, but the practice of discrimination was too strong.

Teams in the Negro Leagues faced major problems, such as finding places to play. The teams often had to rent stadiums from white owners, who didn't always treat them fairly. Many owners did not allow them to use the "white" locker rooms. Nonetheless, the teams persisted, with players playing for the love of the game more than anything else, since most weren't making much money.

The Great Depression in the 1930s marked the end of the early Negro Leagues. Most of the teams, which had a hard time making money, had to call it quits. But touring teams such as the Pittsburgh Crawfords and Washington, DC's Homestead Grays managed to play. Many major leaguers had great respect for the Black ballplayers and still

Youngest Player Ever

In 1944, when most of the country's young men were involved in the war effort, 15-year-old Joe Nuxhall pitched in a game for the Cincinnati Reds to become the youngest major leaguer ever. Nuxhall was quickly sent back down to the minor leagues, but he rejoined the Reds in 1952 and played in the majors for 15 years.

Spahn and Sain

Warren Spahn and Johnny Sain led the pitching staff of the 1948 Boston Braves. Manager Billy Southworth wished he could let them pitch every day. So Gerald V. Hern of *The Boston Post* wrote a poem about them. The poem "Spahn and Sain and Pray for Rain" lives on in baseball's collective memory as a popular slogan for the 1948 Braves.

Hard Ball

Baseball is a game full of action! Fill in as many wild words as you can, using the across and down clues. We left you some T-O-U-G-H letters and words as hints!

ACROSS

3. Fun baseball game played against an upright surface.

6. Team name: Pittsburgh _____.

7. Nickname for a powerful hitter.

11. Smooth, rounded stick used to hit a baseball.

13. The 37-foot-high-wall in Boston's Fenway Park.

16. A "_____ hitter" is a hitter who hits for someone else.

17. To run from one base to another before the next player at bat has hit the ball.

19. Team name: San Francisco _____.

21. If the hitter bunts with a man on third base, it's called a "_____ play."

DOWN

1. Joe DiMaggio's nickname: "_____ in' Joe."

2. When a hitter stops getting hits for a while.

4. Hank Aaron's nickname: "The _____."

5. "The _____" is when fans stand and then sit while moving their arms up and down in a motion that goes all around the stadium.

6. A "_____" fly goes high up in the air and is easily caught.

7. Sharp bumps on the bottom of baseball players' shoes.

8. "The Seventh-Inning _____" gives fans a chance to get up and move around.

9. Team name: Los Angeles _____.

10. The score made by a player who touches first, second, third, and home base.

11. Jose Canseco and Mark McGwire were known as the "_____ Brothers."

12. A ball hit out of fair territory.

14. A _____ play is when a player is trapped between two bases. He has to scramble to get to one base or the other before being tagged out.

15. A "_____ ball" is the speediest pitch.

18. A player will sometimes have to _____ headfirst into a base to avoid being tagged out.

20. A "grand _____" is a home run hit when bases are loaded.

Rookie of the Year

Since Jackie Robinson in 1947, the best first-year player in each league has been honored with the Rookie of the Year award.

fun fact

Why Brooklyn?

New York City consists of five large sections called boroughs. Unlike the Yankees and Giants, the Dodgers claimed to represent only one of these five boroughs, Brooklyn. But in the early days of the Dodgers, Brooklyn by itself had mor people than any other American city except for Chicago!

played exhibition games against these touring teams. By the late 1930s, as the country's economy improved, the Negro Leagues were back with new teams.

In the 1940s, Branch Rickey became determined to sign the first Black major leaguer, despite the negative feelings of the other team owners. Rickey owned the Brooklyn Brown Bombers, a team in the Negro Leagues, and he was also the president and general manager of the Brooklyn Dodgers. In 1945, Rickey watched the Kansas City Monarchs come to town with a young player named Jackie Robinson. Rickey signed Robinson to a minor league contract later that year, and called him up as a member of the Dodgers in 1947.

As more Black players made the major leagues, there was less of a need for the Negro Leagues. While many of the greatest Negro League stars never made it to the major leagues, the leagues gave these ballplayers a place to show their great talents. They would eventually serve as a showcase for players to get to the major leagues. You can't help but wonder how some of the great major leaguers might have fared in daily competition against all of the country's best athletes, not just those who happened to be white.

Famous Negro Leaguer: Satchel Paige, 1926–1953

W-L	ERA	K
28-31	3.29	288

Major league totals only. W-L = wins-losses; ERA = earned run average; K = strikeouts.

Satchel Paige was a genuine baseball superstar. He had a long career, during which an estimated ten million people watched him pitch—in person, since he played most of his games before they were shown on television! Paige played for a variety of Negro League teams from 1926 to 1947, moving from team to team depending on who could pay him the most money. Americans, Black and white, were willing to pay to see Paige pitch. His reputation as one of the greatest pitchers in baseball was well established before World War II, during which he raised money for the war effort through his pitching exhibitions. He played with Negro League all-stars in competitive exhibition games against major leaguers.

Finally, after Jackie Robinson broke in with the Dodgers, Paige was signed to a major league contract with the Cleveland Indians in 1948 at age 42. He played two seasons with the Indians, then moved with owner Bill Veeck to the St. Louis Browns, where he made the all-star team. His career totals look poor compared to the other pitchers listed in this book, but bear in mind that Paige put up these numbers over only five seasons, and he was 47 years old during that last season. One can only imagine the kind of career stats Paige could have earned had he played all of those 27 years in the major leagues.

As more Black players were added to the major leagues, there was less of a need for the Negro Leagues. While many of the greatest Negro League stars never made it to the major leagues, they were accorded Major League status in December 2020 when MLB Commissioner Rob Manfred acknowledged "a longtime oversight." "All of us who love baseball," he said, "have long known that the Negro Leagues produced many of our game's best players, innovations and triumphs against a background of injustice. We are now grateful to count the players of the Negro Leagues where they belong: as Major Leaguers within the official historical record." As a result, the games of the seven Negro Leagues from 1920–1948 are being added to the official statistics and records of Major League Baseball.

Rube Foster

Rube Foster was one of the great pitchers of the early 1900s. He pitched for the 1906 Philadelphia Giants and went on to found the Negro National League, which debuted in 1920 with eight teams. In 1923, Foster helped start a second league with six new teams.

Paige on Age

Satchel Paige, who pitched for nearly 30 years and even appeared in a major league game at the age of 59, once said, "Age is a case of mind over matter. If you don't mind, it don't matter."

1950–1959

World Championships: Yankees (6), New York Giants, Milwaukee Braves, Brooklyn Dodgers, Los Angeles Dodgers

Most Famous Players: Willie Mays, Mickey Mantle, Duke Snider, Ted Williams, Whitey Ford, Stan Musial

The city of New York dominated baseball. Their three teams—the Yankees, the Giants, and the Dodgers—were the best in the game, and they competed for the city's attention. The most memorable moments from those New York rivalries occurred at the end of the 1951 season. The New York Giants and the Brooklyn Dodgers were tied for first place in the NL, so they played a best-of-three playoff to see which team would go to the World Series. The Dodgers led the third game 4–1 going into the bottom of the ninth inning.

The Giants got one run to make the score 4–2, then Bobby Thomson came to bat against pitcher Ralph Branca with two men on base. Thomson hit a home run to left field, winning the game 5–4 and sending the Giants to the World Series. On the radio, Giants announcer Russ Hodges conveyed the fans' excitement with his famous call, shouting over and over, "The Giants win the pennant! The Giants win the pennant!" Thomson's home run became known as the "shot heard round the world."

In the 1950s, refrigerators, washing machines, and other new technologies began to change the way Americans lived. Two new technologies caused lasting changes in major-league baseball. The first was the beginning of televised baseball. Though virtually every game can be seen on television today, in the early 1950s most people didn't even own television sets. But by the end of the decade, millions of people could watch a baseball game even when they couldn't physically go to the game.

It might have been the jet airplane that ended the great New York baseball rivalries. By the end of the 1950s, travel by jet was common, meaning that people could get from the East Coast to the West Coast in less than a day. And, after World War II, the population of California grew very rapidly. To take advantage of the many potential new fans, both the Dodgers and the Giants moved to the West Coast in 1958—the Dodgers to Los Angeles, the Giants to San Francisco.

1960–1969

World Championships: Yankees (2), Dodgers (2), Cardinals (2), Pirates, Orioles, Tigers, Mets

Most Famous Players: Bob Gibson, Sandy Koufax, Don Drysdale, Hank Aaron, Frank Robinson, Willie McCovey, Carl Yastrzemski

New York maintained its reign as the focus of the baseball world, as the Yankees played in the World Series in 1960–1964. Yankee outfielder Roger Maris dueled with teammate Mickey Mantle for the 1961 home run crown—Maris hit number 61 on the last day of the season, breaking Babe Ruth's hallowed record.

The 1960s were a time of expansion. The number of teams in each league hadn't changed for many decades. But in 1961, the American League added two new teams: the Los Angeles Angels and the Washington Senators. A year later, the National League added two new teams: the New York Mets and the Houston Colt .45s, who became the Astros. New teams are usually not very good, and in 1962 the Mets won only forty games while losing 120. This was the worst record ever, and the Mets were greeted with many appropriate jokes.

Baseball expanded by four more teams in 1969: the Montreal Expos and San Diego Padres in the National League, the Seattle Pilots (who became the Milwaukee Brewers after

words to know

pennant

A long, thin, pointed flag—the prize awarded to the teams that win the National League and American League Championship. The two pennant winners play each other in the World Series.

League Championship Series

Until 1969, whichever team won the most regular season games in each league went to the World Series. But starting in 1969, the leagues were split into divisions. The League Championship Series, or LCS, was played between the division winners. So today, the ALCS and the NLCS decide which team in each league goes to the World Series.

just 1 year) and Kansas City Royals in the American League. The twelve-team leagues were each split into two six-team divisions, East and West.

Now you're probably wondering what happened to those terrible Mets. Well, after being pretty dreadful for 7 years, they shocked the world in 1969. The same year that people landed on the moon for the first time ever, the Mets beat the Baltimore Orioles in five games to win the World Series.

1970–1979

World Championships: A's (3), Pirates (2), Reds (2), Yankees (2), Orioles

Most Famous Players: Reggie Jackson, Joe Morgan, Willie Stargell, Tom Seaver, Catfish Hunter, Pete Rose, Johnny Bench

Just 50 or so years ago, the major leagues were very different than they are today. For one thing, players could not be "free agents." Once a player was assigned to a team, he could not change teams unless he was traded or released. In 1972, the major league baseball players went on strike; they won the right to free agency a few years later.

Teams didn't usually score as many runs as they do today, and owners wanted to increase scoring. For example, in the Major Leagues in 1968, teams averaged 3.4 runs per game; in 2019, they averaged 4.8 runs per game. Bob Gibson of the St. Louis Cardinals pitched more than 300 innings in 1968 with a 1.12 ERA. Then, the next year, both leagues lowered the pitching mound from 15 inches to its current height of 10 inches, because it was believed that when a pitcher threw a ball downhill, it was harder for the batter to hit. In response, the American League introduced the "designated hitter" in 1973 to replace at bats by the usually weak-hitting pitchers.

Many teams moved into bigger stadiums in the 1970s, most of which used the same AstroTurf that the Astros put inside their dome. Turf caused the baseball to take high bounces, forcing fielders to adjust their positioning. Speed became a more important part of the game. In 1977, Lou Brock became the first player ever to steal 900 bases, breaking Ty Cobb's previous record of 892. (Rickey Henderson has since passed them both.) Most of these old stadiums were shaped like enormous concrete circles and were also used for football games, concerts, rodeos, and other big events. Tickets were much cheaper than they are now. In those days, a $5 ticket might be considered outrageously expensive; if a $5 ticket is available today, it's as a special discount.

On April 8, 1974, Hammerin' Hank Aaron of the Atlanta Braves hit his 715th career home run, 1 more than Babe Ruth hit. Aaron went on to finish his career where he began it, in Milwaukee, with 755 homers.

Best Record, No Reward

The team with the best record in the 1981 season was the Cincinnati Reds. However, because of the strike and the split season, they didn't make it to the World Series; they didn't even make it to the playoffs. They finished second to the Dodgers in the first half of the season and second to the Astros in the second half.

1980–1989

World Championships: Dodgers (2), Phillies, Cardinals, Orioles, Tigers, Royals, Mets, Twins, A's

Most Famous Players: Ozzie Smith, Nolan Ryan, Dennis Eckersley, Mike Schmidt, George Brett, Wade Boggs, Tony Gwynn, Rickey Henderson

Once players earned the ability to become free agents after their contracts expired, the best of them became objects of bidding wars by owners. In response, owners tried to limit players' abilities to change teams, and baseball players went on strike in the middle of the 1981 season. More than seven hundred games were canceled, and when baseball returned, the season was split into two halves. The winners of the first half played the winners of the second half in a playoff series. Fans were not happy and did not watch much baseball in the second part of the 1981 season.

Baseball recovered as the decade went on. Half of the twenty-six teams played in at least one World Series in the 1980s, and nine different teams won championships. Speed continued to be a critical element of strategy, as pitchers had a hard time preventing the stolen base. In 1981, Rickey Henderson, king of the stolen base, stole a record 130 bases in one season.

The art of base stealing peaked in the 1980s, but the art of relief pitching was only beginning. Until the 1970s, it was normal for the starting pitcher to pitch the whole game. Relief pitchers, whose specific role was to pitch only the late innings, became much more specialized in the 1980s. Most teams began to use a "closer," a relief pitcher with the job of finishing just the last inning or two. Toward the end of the decade, teams began to use "setup" relievers, who relieved the starter in the seventh or eighth inning but gave way to the closer in the ninth.

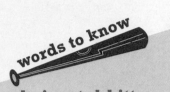

words to know

designated hitter

A player who bats in the lineup instead of the pitcher. The American League uses a designated hitter (DH), but the National League does not—NL pitchers must bat for themselves.

1990–1999

World Championships: Yankees (3), Blue Jays (2), Reds, Twins, Braves, Marlins

Most Famous Players: Greg Maddux, Roger Clemens, Ken Griffey Jr., Randy Johnson, Cal Ripken Jr., Barry Bonds, Mark McGwire

The major leagues expanded even more in the 1990s with the addition of the Florida Marlins, Colorado Rockies, Arizona Diamondbacks, and Tampa Bay Devil Rays. This brought the number of major league teams to today's total of thirty. The league structure was changed once again in 1994, to the present format. Each league was split into three divisions—East, Central, and West.

In 1995, Cal Ripken Jr. of the Orioles played in his 2,131st consecutive game, breaking the record Lou Gehrig set in 1939. The September 6 game drew a sellout crowd, which included the president of the United States, and millions of fans around the world watched on television. Ripken ended his streak in 1998, after playing 2,632 consecutive games.

In one of the saddest episodes in baseball history, a strike ended the 1994 baseball season in August. It was the first time since 1904 that there was no postseason, no World Series, and no championship team. Millionaire players and millionaire team owners got very little sympathy from the fans, who were unhappy that they couldn't watch and enjoy their favorite game. When baseball returned in 1995, attendance was way down. For the next couple of seasons, many fans were turned off to baseball.

In 1997, baseball owners decided that they would try to draw fans back by starting interleague play, which meant regular season games between National and American League teams. Longtime baseball fans weren't happy about it, but on June 12, 1997, the Texas Rangers and the San Francisco Giants played in the first interleague game. What at first appeared to be a novelty caught on as crosstown rivals like the Cubs and White Sox in Chicago, the A's and Giants in neighboring Oakland and San Francisco, and the Mets and Yankees in New York all faced each other during the season.

Starting in the mid-1990s, players hit more home runs than ever before. In 1983, Mike Schmidt hit 40 home runs to lead the league. But in 1996, 40 home runs was only good for twelfth best in the majors. In 1998, two players hit more home runs in the season than ever before. Sammy Sosa hit 66 and Mark McGwire hit 70, both breaking the single-season record of 61 Roger Maris had held since 1961.

There are several possible reasons for this offensive explosion. For one thing, players took weight training more seriously

fun fact

A Family Affair

At one time, Cal Ripken Jr. and his brother, Billy, both played for the Baltimore Orioles, with their dad as coach. In 1987 and 1988, their dad was also the manager.

The Nasty Boys

The Reds of the 1990s used a combination of outstanding relief pitchers. Randy Myers, Rob Dibble, and Norm Charlton regularly held late-inning Reds leads. Two of these three "Nasty Boys," Dibble and Myers, were named Most Valuable Player (MVP) of the 1990 NLCS.

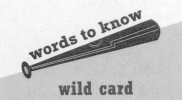

wild card

One of two teams that qualify for postseason games even though they did not end the season at the top of their division. The winner of each division earns a spot in the playoffs, which means there are three teams at the end of the season who will automatically play for the division pennant. Also, a fourth and fifth team in each league play each other in a one-game "wild card" showdown, with the winners advancing to the quarterfinal series. The wild card survivors have the same chance to win the World Series as any other playoff team; in fact, a wild card team won the championship seven times since 1994, most recently the Washington Nationals in 2019.

than ever before. In the 1980s, many teams did not even have their own weight rooms—players on the road had to find a local gym if they wanted to work out. But by the 1990s, teams built gyms, hired athletic trainers, and reaped the benefits of regular workouts. A second possible reason was the league's expansion. The addition of four new teams meant that more than forty pitchers who previously weren't good enough to play in the majors were now pitching to the world's best power hitters.

But in the early 2000s, it came to light that many players were using illegal drugs called anabolic steroids to build their muscles. Sluggers Ken Caminiti and Jose Canseco came forward to tell of their own steroid use and to warn that many others were also using the same drugs. Only a few players directly admitted to using steroids. However, Barry Bonds was investigated by the FBI, and Mark McGwire and Sammy Sosa were called to testify before Congress about their own steroid use. It's still not clear exactly which players were using steroids. But in 2005, the major leagues instituted steroid testing for all players, and players have been hitting fewer home runs than they did two decades ago.

2000–2009

World Championships: Red Sox (2), Yankees (2), Diamondbacks, Angels, Marlins, Cardinals, Phillies, White Sox

Most Famous Players: Pedro Martinez, Derek Jeter, Mariano Rivera, Manny Ramirez, Albert Pujols, Randy Johnson, Ichiro Suzuki, Alex Rodriguez

The terrorist attacks of 2001 put a halt to baseball, but only for a week. The sport, and especially the Yankees' berth in the 2001 World Series, served as a rallying point for American culture. Since 2001, many teams have replaced the traditional singing of "Take Me Out to the Ball Game" during the seventh-inning stretch with "God Bless America."

The Chicago Cubs had not won a World Series since 1908; the Boston Red Sox hadn't won since 1918. Both teams had been considered cursed for as long as most people could remember. In 2003, both teams were very good, and both seemed to have a good chance to make the World Series. But both faltered in the playoffs. The Cubs had to wait a while longer for their championship, but the Red Sox earned their revenge in 2004. In the ALCS, they fell behind the Yankees three games to none, but they came all the way back to win four games to three. Then they swept the St. Louis Cardinals to win their first World Series in 86 years.

Throughout the 2000s, the New York teams spent money like crazy, trying to win by hiring top players. But they couldn't quite seem to beat teams with smaller payrolls. The decade began with a World Series between the Yankees and the Mets in 2000. The Yankees made the playoffs every year from 2000 to 2007 but couldn't win another championship until 2009; the Mets only returned to the playoffs once, and they blew big division leads in both 2007 and 2008. In the 2000s, teams learned that spending money is less important than spending money wisely.

2010–2019

World Championships: Giants (3), Cardinals, Red Sox (2), Royals, Cubs, Astros, Nationals

Most Famous Players: Miguel Cabrera, Buster Posey, Justin Verlander, Bryce Harper, Clayton Kershaw, Mike Trout, Robinson Canó

The San Francisco Giants hadn't won a World Series since they moved to California in the 1950s. But they won in 2010, 2012, and 2014 to become the most dominant baseball fran-

---

fun fact

The Minor Leagues

Each major league team supports several minor league teams, which played through the strike of 1994. Almost every player spends a few years in the minors before coming to the major leagues. Some players are sent back down to the minor leagues if they are not playing well, and sometimes good major-league players will go to the minors after an injury to get used to playing again. Minor league teams are in many smaller cities across the country.

chise since the late-1990s Yankees. Meanwhile, the Giants' archrivals, the Los Angeles Dodgers, filed for bankruptcy and changed owners. The new owners spent a lot of money signing talented players and, with great players such as Justin Turner and three-time Cy Young Award winner Clayton Kershaw, the Dodgers also made the playoffs each year since 2013.

In the American League, the Rangers made the first two World Series appearances in franchise history in consecutive years, but fell short of a championship by a single strike to the Cardinals in 2011.

Two new ballparks opened in the early part of the decade, but neither had a positive impact on their teams. The Twins did earn a third division title in 5 years during their first season at open-air Target Field in Minnesota, but sank to the bottom of the AL Central in following years. Despite the addition of highly paid free agents in 2012, the Marlins suffered through several disastrous seasons at futuristic LoanDepot Park (previously called Marlins Park) and sold off some of their best players before 2013.

In 2015, the Kansas City Royals won their first Series since 1985, just a year after they came up one run short of the title. The Mets took the lead in each of the five games; in four of them, though, the Royals came back to win, including Games 1 and 5 in extra innings.

The following 2 years saw two teams that had gone a while without winning finally get that World Series championship. In 2016, after 108 years since their last championship, the Chicago Cubs won the World Series. In 2017, for the first time in franchise history, the Houston Astros won the championship. It was especially important for the Astros, as Houston had been hit by a devastating hurricane just two months before the Series began.

Say What?

Yogi Berra was known as quite a talker behind the plate. He hoped his chatter would distract the batter! The story goes that in the 1958 World Series, with the legendary Hank Aaron hitting, Yogi kept telling Aaron to "hit with the label up on the bat." Finally, Aaron couldn't stand it anymore. He turned to Yogi and said " _____!"

To find out what Hank Aaron said to Yogi Berra, figure out where to put each of the cut-apart pieces of the grid.

C'mon Hank, hit it with the label up. Up, up, up, with the label up. C'mon Hank, hit it with the label up...

41

The Pace of the Game

One of the beauties of baseball is that the game has no clock. But a game that used to take 2 or 2.5 hours to play now routinely takes more than 3 hours to complete. Pitchers and batters tend to take longer and longer to get ready for action; numerous pitching changes and replay delays add time onto the game. Starting in 2015, Major League Baseball began to enforce rules about time between innings, and batters and pitchers taking too long. No one minds long games with lots of action, but it's difficult for fans to watch pitchers think for 45 seconds about their next pitch when it's already 11:00 at night.

2020–2021

World Championships: Dodgers, Braves

Most Famous Players: Shohei Ohtani, Vladimir Guerrero Jr., Fernando Tatis Jr., Juan Soto, Corey Seager, Jacob deGrom, Trea Turner, Freddie Freeman

The most remarkable achievement of the 2020 season was that it happened at all. Set against the background of the COVID-19 pandemic, major league baseball and its players agreed to a sixty-game regular season without fans in the stands. Temporary rules were introduced, such as seven-inning games for doubleheaders, universal designated hitters, and a sixteen-team playoff system. Also, if a game went into extra innings, the innings began with a runner on second base. The World Series between the Dodgers and Rays was the first ever played at a neutral site, Globe Life Field in Arlington, Texas. About 11,500 spectators were allowed to attend.

When fans returned in 2021, they got to witness a historic season created by the achievements of Japanese-born Shohei Ohtani. The Angels' breakout star not only hit massive home runs but became an overpowering starting pitcher—he hit his 36th home run on the night after he struck out his 100th batter. Not even the iconic Babe Ruth attempted to dominate as both hitter and pitcher in the same season. Additionally, Vladimir Guerrero Jr. and Fernando Tatis Jr., both only 22 years old, electrified the sport with their batting talents.

Competitively, the 2021 season was remarkable. The Giants won a franchise-record 107 games, yet finished only one game ahead of the Dodgers in the NL West. Four teams remained in contention for the two AL wild card spots on the final day of the regular season. And the World Series was won by the playoff team with the least impressive record, the Braves (88–73).

Chapter 3
The National League

Baseball today is played by all sorts of teams: youth leagues, high school districts, college conferences, semipro leagues, and minor leagues. The best-known teams play in the major leagues: the National League and the American League. Some of these teams, like the Dodgers and Yankees, have been around since well before even your great-grandparents were born. Others are less than 30 years old. In this chapter, you can read about every National League team—including, maybe, your favorite team.

The Start of the National League

In the 1870s, the National Association, one of the first professional baseball leagues, was having trouble. The team owners weren't following the league rules. The Boston Red Stockings seemed to win all the time. There was some shady business with gamblers who might have been fixing games. William Hulbert, owner of the Chicago White Stockings, convinced seven other owners to join with him in a new league: the National League. Only two of the teams—the Cubs and the Braves—are still playing today.

The Original 1876 National League

1876 Team Name	Modern Team Name
Chicago White Stockings	Chicago Cubs
Philadelphia Athletics	The Philadelphia Athletics only played in the NL in 1876
Boston Red Stockings	Atlanta Braves
Hartford Dark Blues	The Hartford Dark Blues only played in the NL in 1876 and 1877
Mutual of New York	Mutual of New York only played in the NL in 1876

St. Louis Brown Stockings	The St. Louis Brown Stockings only played in the NL in 1876 and 1877
Cincinnati Red Stockings	The Cincinnati Red Stockings only played in the NL from 1876 to 1880
Louisville Grays	The Louisville Grays only played in the NL in 1876 and 1877

Teams frequently joined and left the National League, especially in its early years. The National League got up to sixteen teams from 1997 to 2013; in 2013, the Houston Astros switched to the American League, leaving fifteen teams in each league.

San Francisco Giants

Founded in 1883
Other names: New York Gothams, New York Giants
8 World Championships (1905, 1921, 1922, 1933, 1954, 2010, 2012, 2014)
23 NL pennants

Even though the Giants have played in San Francisco for more than 60 years, they enjoyed championship seasons in four different decades while representing New York. During that time, their foremost rivals were the crosstown Brooklyn Dodgers. Both teams moved to California following the 1957 season.

Although the Dodgers won a World Championship in their second year on the West Coast, the Giants had to wait, and wait some more. Despite eight previous trips to the

---

fun fact

The Windiest Ballpark

Candlestick Park, which was the home of the Giants for 40 years before the construction of Oracle Park in 2000, was built in an unsheltered area along San Francisco Bay. Candlestick was known for being very windy and cold, even in the summer. If you watch any old Giants games there, you'll see hot dog wrappers (and fly balls) blowing all over the place and fans huddling under blankets. In the midst of the 1961 All-Star Game at Candlestick, the skinny relief pitcher Stu Miller was stopped midpitch by a gust of wind.

playoffs and three previous World Series appearances while representing San Francisco, it took the Giants more than a half-century to claim their first championship in California. They enjoyed it so much that they won twice more in the next 4 years.

Soon after their breakthrough in 2010, the Giants won again in 2012 and 2014, thanks to exceptional pitching performances. Tim Lincecum, who won two games as a starter in the 2010 Series, pitched almost five innings of scoreless relief in the 2012 Series, leading to a four-game sweep over the Tigers. Even better, Madison Bumgarner, who was a winner in one of the two Giants' shutouts in 2012, allowed only one run in three appearances covering twenty-one innings (two wins and one save) in 2014 during the seven-game triumph over the Royals. A common thread among the championship teams was the presence of catcher Buster Posey, Rookie of the Year (2010), Most Valuable Player (2012), and a .300-plus hitter in all three seasons. In his final season (2021), he led the Giants to a franchise-record 107 wins.

"He's Always There"

Former Dodgers player and manager Gil Hodges talked about how good a defensive player Willie Mays really was: "I can't very well tell my hitters, don't hit it to him. Wherever they hit it, he's always there."

Famous Giant: Willie Mays, 1951–1973

HR	RBI	AVG
660	1,903	.302

He was known as the "Say Hey Kid" and was one of the greatest and most likable players to ever play the game. After his rookie season in 1951, Mays spent 2 years in the army before returning to the (then New York) Giants, with whom he racked up 41 homers and won the World Championship over the Cleveland Indians.

Willie could do it all. He hit for power, leading the league in homers four times, and he also had great speed, leading the league in stolen bases four times. He was known for incredible defense; with his basket catch, he used the glove as a "basket" to catch fly balls at his waist. Perhaps the most famous catch Mays ever made came in the first game of the 1954 World Series, as he grabbed a ball going over his head in the deepest part of center field to help the Giants hold on and win. After many years with the Giants in San Francisco, Mays spent his last couple of years back in New York with the Mets before retiring as the third-greatest home run hitter ever. A baseball legend, Mays made the Hall of Fame in 1979.

Amazing Mays

A Giants broadcaster, in awe of one of Mays's hits, said, "The only player who could have caught that ball, hit it."

Philadelphia Phillies

Founded in 1883
Other names: Philadelphia Quakers, Philadelphia Blue Jays
2 World Championships (1980, 2008)
7 NL pennants

The Phillies' last World Championship, in 2008, occurred in the same season they achieved something less memorable: They lost a game for the 10,000th time in club history, a record for an American sports franchise. The franchise has had more than its share of bad years—twice in its history, the Phillies have gone more than a decade without a winning season.

But the twenty-first century has been the best of times for the team. Not only did the Phillies upgrade their home park from multipurpose Veterans Stadium, with its rock-hard artificial turf, to beautiful baseball-only Citizens Bank Park; they also reeled off five consecutive division titles, including back-to-back trips to the World Series in 2008 and 2009. Behind the hitting of Ryan Howard and Chase Utley, and the relief pitching of Brad Lidge, who was a perfect 41-for-41 in save situations during the regular season

Who Was the Most Famous Giant?

In this chapter, you'll read short notes about famous players on some teams. But since baseball has been around for such a long time, there are way more players than there is room to write about them. If you want to learn more about famous players on your favorite team, check out Baseball-Reference.com.

and 7-for-7 in the postseason, the Phillies won their second championship in 2008.

Boo!

Philadelphia is known as a tough town in which to be a sports star. The fans take pride in yelling "Boo!" all the time. In fact, even though Phillies fans worship Mike Schmidt as one of their town's best professional athletes ever, the Veterans Stadium crowd once booed him. But that shouldn't make him feel too bad—Philadelphia fans famously booed Santa Claus at a football game!

Famous Phillie: Mike Schmidt, 1972–1989

HR	RBI	AVG
548	1,595	.267

Many baseball fans consider Mike Schmidt to be the best all-around third baseman ever to play the game. He was a truly awesome power hitter, leading the league eight times in home runs. In just 17 years he placed himself among the top ten all-time leaders in homers, won three MVPs, and helped lead the Phillies to their first ever World Championship. On the other side of the field, he was a tremendous defensive player. He won the Gold Glove as the best fielding third baseman in the National League nine times. He went about his business very seriously, and fans and players alike respected and admired his talent and his work ethic. Schmidt retired in 1989 and was elected to the Hall of Fame in 1995.

Colorado Rockies

Founded in 1993
0 World Championships
1 NL pennant

The Rockies were an unusual team from the beginning, simply because of where they play. Denver, Colorado, is known as the Mile High City because it is located more than 5,000 feet (about a mile) above sea level. Why is this important? At high altitudes, breaking balls don't curve very much, which makes them easier to hit, and batted balls fly farther.

For the first 9 years of the team's existence, Rockies home games were nearly always slugfests. From 1995 to 2001, Coors Field saw an average of 13.8 runs and 3.2 home runs *per game*! Since 2002, the Rockies have stored their baseballs in a specially made humidor that cost $15,000. The humidor controls temperature and humidity so the balls won't be damaged by Denver's low humidity, and run scoring at Coors has gone way down as a result.

Through their first decade, the Rockies focused on finding the best sluggers. The "Blake Street Bombers," led by Andrés Galarraga, put the Rockies in the playoffs in 1995. After the introduction of the humidor, the team developed some excellent pitchers. They made their second playoff appearance in 2007 after winning fourteen of their last fifteen regular season games. They made it to the World Series but were swept by the Boston Red Sox for the championship. Led by Nolan Arenado, a power hitter who earned eight Gold Gloves as a third baseman, the Rockies returned to the playoffs in 2017 and 2018 but they failed to win a game. They traded Arenado to the Cardinals following the 2020 season.

St. Louis Cardinals

Founded in 1882
Other names: St. Louis Brown Stockings, St. Louis Browns, St. Louis Perfectos
11 World Championships (1926, 1931, 1934, 1942, 1944, 1946, 1964, 1967, 1982, 2006, 2011)
19 NL pennants

The Cardinals' eleven World Series titles are the most in National League history, and second overall behind the Yankees. But the Cardinals' beginnings were modest. Founded as the St. Louis Brown Stockings, they were expelled from the

Curt Flood: Hero of the Players

In 1969, the Cardinals traded 12-year veteran, Gold Glove outfielder Curt Flood to the Phillies. But Flood didn't want to accept the trade—he asked the commissioner to allow him to choose a team for himself. When the commissioner refused, Flood sued, and his case went all the way to the Supreme Court. Flood lost his case eventually and sat out of baseball for a year. But with Flood's influence, the players' union kept pushing for and eventually won the right for players to be "free agents"—to sign with any club they choose.

National League after 2 years for a game-fixing scandal. Entering the American Association as the Browns in 1882, they quickly rose to the top, but the AA disbanded following the 1891 season. Rejoining the NL in 1892, they sank to the bottom of the standings, and remained in that vicinity until 1919.

The revival of the franchise, which changed its name to the Cardinals in 1900, began with the arrival of Branch Rickey. As business manager, the former catcher started the practice of buying minor league clubs to serve as farm teams. Players promoted from that system served as the core of the team that lifted the Cardinals to their first World Championship in 1926, and to five more over the next 20 years. Boasting such great players as Joe Medwick, Dizzy Dean, and Stan "The Man" Musial, whose statue stands outside Busch Stadium, the Cardinals won nine pennants, and suffered only three losing seasons between 1921 and 1946.

In the past 40 years, the franchise has been similarly successful, if not as consistent. Whitey Herzog managed the Cardinals to three World Series appearances in the 1980s, with the team built for speed on the artificial turf of the old multipurpose Busch Stadium. Taking over as manager in 1996, Tony La Russa led the team to the playoffs in nine of his sixteen seasons, including World Championships in 2006 and 2011, both in the new, retro-styled Busch Stadium. Following La Russa's retirement, the Cardinals advanced to the postseason seven times in the next decade, winning a franchise-record seventeen consecutive games in September to qualify as a wild card in 2021.

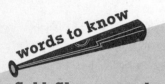

words to know

Gold Glove award

An award for fielding excellence given every year to the best fielder at each position in both the National and American League.

Famous Cardinal: Albert Pujols, 2001–

HR	RBI	AVG
679	2,150	.297

If he had retired the moment he removed his Cardinals' uniform in 2011, Albert Pujols still would be a lock for the Hall of Fame. The greatest single offensive force of the twenty-first century, he remains the only player in history to bat .300 or better, hit 30 home runs, and drive in at least 100 runs in each of his first ten major league seasons. Born in the Dominican Republic but raised in Missouri, the thirteenth round draft pick managed to win Rookie of the Year and three Most Valuable Player awards while leading St. Louis to a pair of World Series championships. After ten additional seasons with the Angels and Dodgers, he ranks fifth on the all-time home run list and third in RBIs behind only Hank Aaron and Babe Ruth.

An Early Sign of Greatness

Albert Pujols played only 1 year in college at Maple Woods Community College in Kansas City, where he hit 22 home runs and had a batting average of .466. In his first ever college game, he hit a grand slam and turned an unassisted triple play. An unassisted triple play is so rare, it's only been done fifteen times in Major League Baseball. And he wasn't even in the major leagues yet!

Miami Marlins

Founded in 1993
Other names: Florida Marlins
2 World Championships (1997, 2003)
2 NL pennants

Even though they have only been around since 1993, the Marlins have already won two World Championships. For the first, in 1997, the team signed many star players who earned big salaries. Despite their World Series victory over the Cleveland Indians, their owner decided he couldn't afford to keep paying his stars. So he held a fire sale, trading most of his best players. That left the Marlins among the worst teams in baseball, and they didn't manage another winning season until 2003.

The good news was that several of the young players acquired in those drastic trades and in the annual amateur draft matured and, under the skillful direction of Jack McKeon, surged to surprising victories over the Giants and

Cubs in the 2003 NL playoffs and the Yankees in the World Series, capped by Josh Beckett's complete-game shutout in Game 6 at Yankee Stadium. Later, the Marlins, under different ownership, again chose to break up the team.

The only positive development for the team since then has been the opening of a futuristic baseball-only stadium in 2012. The Marlins have endured tragedy with the accidental boating death of pitching star José Fernández in September 2016, and questionable decisions with the trades of reigning MVP Giancarlo Stanton to the Yankees and future MVP Christian Yelich to the Brewers one month apart following the 2017 season.

Arizona Diamondbacks

Founded in 1998
1 World Championship (2001)
1 NL pennant

Although the Diamondbacks are the youngest National League team, they reached the playoffs in five of their first fifteen seasons, and won a dramatic seven-game World Series against the defending champion Yankees in 2001. They also experienced four last-place finishes in the NL West before returning to contention in recent years.

The Diamondbacks play in Chase Field, a big, quirky ballpark with a retractable roof and a pool behind the right field fence to combat the desert heat. The center field fence is tall and very deep. The team has always put outstanding pitchers on the mound, taking advantage of the large field. Curt Schilling and Randy Johnson were co-MVPs of the 2001 World Series; Brandon Webb was among the top pitchers of the decade. A postseason participant as recently as 2017 and a contender even after the trade of all-star first baseman

Paul Goldschmidt to the Cardinals following the 2018 season, the Diamondbacks hit bottom in 2021 when they set a modern major league record by losing twenty-four consecutive road games.

New York Mets

Founded in 1962
2 World Championships (1969, 1986)
5 NL pennants

After both the Dodgers and the Giants left New York for California following the 1957 season, National League fans wanted a replacement team. They didn't want to root for the hated Yankees, the only remaining New York team. So the Mets, adopting the colors of the departing franchises—blue for the Dodgers and orange for the Giants—were formed as an expansion team in 1962.

In their first season, the Mets were genuinely awful, compiling a 40-120 record. However, because they featured some of the Dodgers' and Giants' old heroes, and because the beloved and entertaining Casey Stengel managed them, they were embraced by the fans. After 7 years of dismal finishes, just as New York was growing impatient with the results, the Mets suddenly blossomed in the midst of the 1969 season. Behind the standout pitching of Tom Seaver and Jerry Koosman, and under the even-handed direction of manager Gil Hodges (an original Met), the team rallied to overcome the heavily favored Cubs in the first year of division play, sweep the Braves in the NLCS, and stun a great Baltimore Orioles team for a World Championship that was deemed a miracle.

The sudden death of Hodges in the spring of 1972 cast a pall over the franchise, although the Mets did squeeze out a second World Series appearance in 1973, despite the worst

The Big Unit Was Scary!

Randy Johnson, the 6'10" lefty known as the "Big Unit," won five Cy Young Awards. In the 1993 All-Star Game, the Phillies' best hitter, left-hander John Kruk, stepped up against Randy Johnson for the first time. Kruk was completely intimidated. He ducked and backed away from three straight pitches even though all three were strikes.

record (82-79) of any team to qualify for the Fall Classic. It would be more than a decade before they made it back, riding the arm of Dwight Gooden, the leadership of Keith Hernandez and Gary Carter, and a favorable bounce to a memorable World Championship in 1986.

In 2000, the Mets played in the first postseason Subway Series in 44 years, a losing showdown against the Yankees. However, historic collapses cost the Mets the pennant in 2007 and a playoff berth on the last day of the season in 2008, after which not even a move from Shea Stadium to sparkling Citi Field in 2009 could prevent a decline. The promotion of three young starting pitchers—Jacob deGrom, Matt Harvey, and Noah Syndergaard—and a bolt of offensive energy from Yoenis Céspedes catapulted the Mets to the 2015 World Series, which they lost to the Royals. The decade ended on a positive note when billionaire and longtime fan Steve Cohen bought the team in September 2020.

words to know

Cy Young Award

The award given every year to the best pitcher in each league. It's named after the pitcher with the most wins in baseball history.

Famous Met: Tom Seaver, 1967–1986

W-L	ERA	K
311-205	2.86	3,640

When "Tom Terrific" came up with the New York Mets in 1967, the Mets were the worst team in the major leagues. By 1969, they shocked everyone and won 100 games, with Tom Seaver winning 25 of them on the way to a World Championship. Seaver won his first of three Cy Young Awards that year and became the heart and soul of the Mets. In 1973, he led the Mets back to the World Series, but this time they lost to the A's. Much to the disappointment of Mets fans, he was traded away in 1977, returning only for a brief stint before his retirement in 1986. In his career, he won 20 or more games four times and led the league in strikeouts

Play Ball

A baseball player must be sure to follow the rules of the game, or he could get sent to the dugout! You must carefully follow the directions below to learn the words that finish the following popular saying: "Some people say that playing baseball is as American as eating _____."

1. Print the word BASEBALL. **BASEBALL**

2. Switch the position of the first two letters. *ABSBE*

3. Move the 5th letter between the 2nd and 3rd letters. *ABSBE*

4. Switch the positions of the 4th and 8th letters.

5. Change the 6th letter to P.

6. Change the last letter to E.

7. Change both B's to P's.

8. Change the 7th letter to I.

five times. Seaver retired as one of the twenty winningest pitchers of all time, and he sits sixth all-time in strikeouts. He was elected to the Hall of Fame in 1992 and returned to the Mets one more time—this time as an announcer.

Atlanta Braves

Founded in 1876
Other names: Boston Red Stockings, Boston Red Caps, Boston Beaneaters, Boston Doves, Boston Rustlers, Boston Bees, Boston Braves, Milwaukee Braves
4 World Championships (1914, 1957, 1995, 2021)
18 NL pennants

The only franchise to win a World Championship in three different cities, the Braves started out in Boston. They were very, very good in the nineteenth century, winning eight pennants between 1876 and 1899. They won the World Series in 1914, but weren't contenders again until the late 1940s.

The team moved to Milwaukee in 1953, and then became the first major league team to represent the South in 1966. The Braves were the joke of the National League through much of the 1970s and 1980s. However, in 1990 the team hired general manager John Schuerholz away from Kansas City. Schuerholz signed Bobby Cox as his manager, and Cox named Leo Mazzone his pitching coach. Under their leadership, the Braves dominated the league in the 1990s. With phenomenal starting pitching, they won their division every year between 1991 and 2005, wresting the World Series title in 1995 from the Cleveland Indians. After Cox's retirement in 2010, the Braves have won five division titles and added an unlikely world championship in 2021 under Brian Snitker.

Mazzone on Pitching

Most starting pitchers are afraid to throw too much between starts for fear of hurting their arms. Braves pitching coach Leo Mazzone thought that was ridiculous. He had his pitchers throw off the mound twice between starts, though only at about half speed. He seemed to know what he was doing because the Braves had the best starting pitching in the majors for more than a decade.

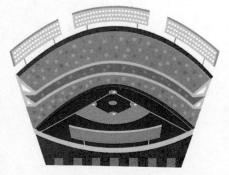

Famous Brave: Hank Aaron, 1954–1976

HR	RBI	AVG
755	2,297	.305

Many people thought Babe Ruth's record of 714 career home runs would never be broken. Hank Aaron, nicknamed "the Hammer," knew better. Aaron played briefly in the Negro Leagues before being signed in 1954 by the Milwaukee Braves, who moved to Atlanta in 1966.

Aaron never topped 50 homers in a season, but he belted at least 25 home runs eighteen times, with a high of 47. He also posted more than 120 RBIs seven times while setting the all-time career RBI record. By the time he finished his 23-year career back in Milwaukee as a member of the Brewers, he was also near the top in games played, hits, runs scored, and doubles. Aaron made the Hall of Fame in 1982.

Famous Brave: Greg Maddux, 1986–2008

W-L	ERA	K
355-227	3.16	3,371

He didn't have the blazing fastball of Randy Johnson, and he never led the major leagues in strikeouts, but his secret to pitching was, as he put it, "making your strikes look like balls and your balls look like strikes." Greg Maddux was a very smart pitcher with tremendous control who knew how to get batters out. In 1997, for example, he walked only twenty batters in over 230 innings. He knew how to throw several pitches very well, and he could hit the corners of the plate with all of them. In 1995 and 1996, with the Braves, Maddux went a combined 35-8 with a 1.60 ERA, capturing two of his four Cy Young Awards; in fact, some people in the late 1990s joked about renaming the award the "Greg Maddux Award." Maddux made the Hall of Fame in 2014.

San Diego Padres

Founded in 1969
0 World Championships
2 NL pennants

The expansion Padres posted only one winning record over their first fifteen seasons. However, not only did they win 92 games in 1984, but they also won their division and the pennant, rallying behind young Tony Gwynn and veteran Steve Garvey to overcome a 2–0 deficit in the best-of-five NLCS against the Cubs. They staged a similar rise in 1998, propelled once again by Gwynn, then 38 and an eight-time batting champion. On both occasions, the Padres were overwhelmed in the World Series, first by the Tigers and then the Yankees, winning a combined total of one game.

Bruce Bochy, the backup catcher on the 1984 Padres, managed the team in 1998. He also managed the club in the next three seasons in which it qualified for the playoffs—1996, 2005, and 2006. He left in 2007 to manage the Giants, who won the World Series in 2010, 2012, and 2014. Meanwhile, the Padres lapsed into rebuilding mode until the free agent signing of Manny Machado and the development of electrifying shortstop Fernando Tatis Jr. lifted the team into the expanded 2020 playoffs and the role of future contender.

Famous Padre: Tony Gwynn, 1982–2001

HR	RBI	AVG
135	1,138	.338

fun fact

Brothers Who Hit Home Runs

There have been many brothers who played major league baseball, from Joe, Vince, and Dom DiMaggio to Cal and Billy Ripken to Aaron and Bret Boone. But who were the brothers who hit the most combined home runs? Hank and Tommie Aaron. Hammerin' Hank hit 755, while Tommie added on 13 for a grand total of 768.

From the moment he came up to the big leagues, Gwynn was the best hitter in baseball and one of the best of all time. His career .338 average is up there with the greats of the early 1900s, and in 1994 he came within 6 points of batting .400, something that hadn't been done since 1941. Gwynn led the league in batting seven times, hitting over .360 four times. He could hit any pitch for a single or double and hardly ever struck out, which helps explain why he had over 3,000 career hits. In his younger years he was also a great base stealer and tremendous defensive player. Gwynn retired at the end of the 2001 season after 20 years with the San Diego Padres and nineteen consecutive .300 seasons. He was inducted into the Hall of Fame in 2007. His son, Tony Gwynn Jr., played two seasons for the Padres.

Cincinnati Reds

Founded in 1882
Other names: Cincinnati Red Stockings, Cincinnati Redlegs
5 World Championships (1919, 1940, 1975, 1976, 1990)
9 NL pennants

The original Cincinnati Red Stockings team was formed in 1863. Five years later, they became the first professional baseball team, composed entirely of players paid a salary by the team owner. That team lasted until 1870. A new Cincinnati Red Stockings team joined the National League in 1876 but was kicked out of the league. So today's Reds are really the third team to represent Cincinnati in professional baseball.

The Reds' first World Championship, in 1919, was clouded by the "Black Sox" scandal, in which gamblers paid members of the Chicago White Sox to lose the World Series. The most famous Reds teams dominated the 1970s, when they were known as the "Big Red Machine." Johnny Bench,

Pete Rose, Joe Morgan, Tony Pérez, and George Foster formed the core of a fearsome batting order for manager Sparky Anderson. From 1961 to 1981, the Reds reeled off nineteen winning seasons and seven playoff appearances.

After a few tough seasons at the start of the 1980s, the Reds improved under the direction of hometown hero Pete Rose. He was relieved as manager in 1989 after being accused of betting on baseball games and was followed by Lou Piniella, who led the Reds to a World Series sweep of the defending champion Oakland A's in 1990. The Reds became consistent playoff contenders again under manager Dusty Baker, largely through the offensive efforts of Joey Votto and Brandon Phillips, but have yet to win a playoff series in the twenty-first century.

Famous Red: Johnny Bench, 1967–1983

HR	RBI	AVG
389	1,376	.267

There was never a greater major league catcher than Johnny Bench. He broke into the major leagues in style when he was just 20 years old, making the All-Star Game and winning Rookie of the Year honors. In 1970, his third season, Bench won the National League MVP with 45 homers and 148 RBIs while leading the Reds to the World Series. Bench topped the 100 RBI mark on five occasions and was the main cog in Cincinnati's "Big Red Machine."

Besides his tremendous power hitting and many clutch hits, Bench was also an incredible defensive catcher and was known for his great throwing arm. He won ten Gold Glove awards as the best defensive catcher in the National League until injuries forced him to spend more time at third and first base. Two World Championships and consistently good play made Johnny Bench one of baseball's most popular players of the 1970s. But the injuries from catching caught up with him, and at age 35 Bench had to call it quits. He was elected to the Hall of Fame in 1989.

Los Angeles Dodgers

Founded in 1884
Other names (all from their Brooklyn days): Brooklyn Atlantics, Grays, Grooms, Bridegrooms, Superbas, Robins, Dodgers
7 World Championships (1955, 1959, 1963, 1965, 1981, 1988, 2020)
24 NL pennants

words to know

player-manager

A manager of a team who is also a player. Hiring a player to manage the team used to be more common than it is now. The most recent player-manager was Pete Rose, who played for and managed the Reds in 1985 and 1986.

While the Dodgers occupied their original home of Brooklyn, New York, they made it to the World Series nine times—the last seven against the New York Yankees—but won only in 1955. Just 2 years after their lone championship, Brooklyn fans were heartbroken to see their "Bums," as they were fondly called, move thousands of miles away to Los Angeles.

But Southern California embraced its new team, and the Dodgers won a World Series in only their second season on the West Coast, in 1959. After 4 years in the misshapen Los Angeles Memorial Coliseum, they moved into a beautiful new stadium in 1962, and reached the World Series in 3 of the next 4 years.

The Dodgers have historically been one of the best-run clubs in baseball. Great pitchers have been at the heart of the team's success, from Hall of Famers Sandy Koufax and Don Drysdale in the 1960s, to Fernando Valenzuela and Orel Hershiser in the 1980s, to Clayton Kershaw, who capped a brilliant career with two victories in the 2020 World Series triumph over the Rays. Their 2021 payroll, the most expensive in the majors, included four Cy Young Award winners and four Most Valuable Players.

Famous Dodger: Jackie Robinson, 1947–1956

HR	RBI	AVG
137	734	.311

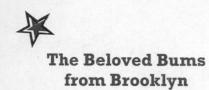

The Beloved Bums from Brooklyn

Many people used to get around New York City by taking the trolley, which was a sort of train that ran at street level. People had to dodge the trolleys as they crossed streets—hence, the baseball team became the Brooklyn Trolley Dodgers. But fans sometimes referred to their team simply as the "Bums."

Jackie Robinson broke into the major leagues with the Brooklyn Dodgers in 1947 at the age of 28 after a year in the Negro Leagues and 2 years in the minors. He led the league in stolen bases and won Rookie of the Year honors. But his entry into the majors was far more significant than his stats. Robinson broke the color barrier, becoming the first Black player to play in the major leagues, at least since the late 1800s. Making a major statement for his race wasn't new to Robinson, who had been court-martialed out of the United States Army after he had refused to sit in the back of a bus because of the color of his skin.

The early days of his career were very difficult. Fans, players on other teams, and even many of his own teammates were cruel. Some players even started a petition that said they would not play in the game with him. But there were a lot of people on his side. He got support from some of his teammates, the Dodgers' manager and front office, and even the baseball commissioner. He also had the support and hopes of Black Americans, who rooted passionately for him—even if he was playing against their own team! He also showed a great deal of sheer determination and proved himself as a first-rate ballplayer.

In 1949, Robinson hit .342, which led the league in batting, and he was named the MVP. In the next 10 years he would make a huge breakthrough for the game of baseball. Robinson's legacy continued long after his seven World Series appearances and his induction into the Hall of Fame in 1962. In 1997, stadiums all over the country honored the 50-year anniversary of Robinson's achievement. His uniform number, 42, was retired throughout major league baseball.

Though Jackie Robinson will be remembered foremost for breaking baseball's color barrier, it must be noted that his performance earned him recognition as one of the all-time greatest players of any color.

Switch Hitter

Can you see the ten differences between the two pictures of this batter?

HINT: It doesn't count that he's facing in different directions—that's what a switch hitter does!

Milwaukee Brewers

Founded in 1969
Other names: Seattle Pilots
0 World Championships
1 AL pennant; 0 NL pennants

In 1969, the American League granted membership to two expansion teams, the Kansas City Royals and the Seattle Pilots. The Pilots, playing their first season in a minor league ballpark, went bankrupt. They were sold to Bud Selig, a Milwaukee car dealer who had been a minor shareholder in the Braves before they left town for Atlanta. He renamed them the Brewers, and controlled the franchise until he was appointed commissioner of baseball in 1992.

The Brewers were rarely contenders in the AL, or in the National League after they switched to it following the 1997 season. They did make the playoffs in the split season of 1981, and represented the AL in the 1982 World Series with a team of sluggers branded "Harvey's Wallbangers" in honor of manager Harvey Kuenn. However, their next postseason appearance didn't occur until 2008. With a team featuring Prince Fielder and Most Valuable Player Ryan Braun, they won their first NL division series and first NL playoff series in 2011 before falling to the Cardinals in the NLCS. In his first season with the Brewers, Christian Yelich won the NL MVP award in 2018 and helped elevate the team to the top of the Central Division. In losing to the Dodgers in the NLCS, Milwaukee fell one game short of the World Series, but the team remains a championship contender.

Pittsburgh Pirates

Founded in 1892
Other names: Pittsburgh Alleghenys
5 World Championships (1909, 1925, 1960, 1971, 1979)
9 NL pennants

The Pirates reached their peak in the 1970s, when they rivaled the Cincinnati "Big Red Machine" as the team of the decade. While the franchise shifted from historic Forbes Field to Three Rivers Stadium, and leadership passed from the late, great Roberto Clemente to slugger Willie Stargell, the Pirates made six appearances in the playoffs. They won the World Series in 1971, with Clemente in a starring role, and in 1979, with Stargell overseeing a joyous group that chose the disco hit "We Are Family" as its theme song.

It was a decade before the Pirates returned to the playoffs. A young Barry Bonds led Pittsburgh to the National League Championship Series in 3 consecutive years, but the Pirates' hopes came crashing down in Game 7 of the 1992 series, when the Braves scored 3 runs in the bottom of the ninth inning to clinch a second straight National League pennant. Bonds's throw to the plate was just late as Sid Bream slid across with the winning run on Francisco Cabrera's single.

Bonds left for San Francisco as a free agent the following season, and the Pirates slipped into oblivion. The only positive development in the next 20 years was the opening of beautiful PNC Park, facing the Allegheny River and the city's skyscrapers, in 2001. However, the patient hand of manager Clint Hurdle paid off in 2013, when young stars Andrew McCutchen and Pedro Álvarez led the team to the playoffs. They have not returned since 2015.

Who's Who?

Some baseball nicknames are easy to guess. For example, almost all players who have had the last name "Rhodes" have gotten the nickname "Dusty." See how many of the famous nicknames on the left you can match with the real names on the right. Put the number of the correct nickname on the line in front of each real name.

1. The Big Train
2. Tom Terrific
3. Cyclone
4. Jotlin' Joe
5. Double X
6. Mr. October
7. The Mick
8. Say Hey Kid
9. Stan The Man
10. Charlie Hustle
11. Wizard of Oz
12. The Big Unit
13. The Rocket

____ Cy Young
____ Jimmy Foxx
____ Joe DiMaggio
____ Mickey Mantle
____ Ozzie Smith
____ Pete Rose
____ Randy Johnson
____ Reggie Jackson
____ Roger Clemons
____ Stan Musial
____ Tom Seaver
____ Walter Johnson
____ Willie Mays

Look! It's "Bubbles" MacCoy!

Famous Pirate: Roberto Clemente, 1955–1972

HR	RBI	AVG
240	1,305	.317

Roberto Clemente was a tremendous all-around ball-player. Not only could he hit for a high average; he also had power and was a super defensive outfielder, winning twelve Gold Gloves. He joined the Pirates in the mid-1950s as a 20-year-old rookie from Puerto Rico. He went on to become the greatest player from Puerto Rico and the first Hispanic player elected to the Hall of Fame in 1973. Clemente led the National League in batting four times in the 1960s, and four times he had more than 200 hits in a season. He appeared in two World Series for the Pirates and batted .362 overall, helping lead the Pirates to the title in 1971.

Clemente became one of the few players to get his 3,000th hit, which came at the end of the 1972 season. It would be his last hit ever. On December 31, 1972, he was on his way to deliver supplies to victims of a severe earthquake in Nicaragua when the plane he was on crashed. Clemente died at age 38 but is remembered as a hero both on and off the field.

Washington Nationals

Founded in 1969
Other names: Montreal Expos
1 World Championship (2019)
1 NL pennant

After years of playing bad baseball as the Montreal Expos, the team moved to Washington, DC, and changed their name to the Nationals. They continued to struggle for a while, but began to build a great minor league system. In 2019, behind homegrown stars like pitcher Stephen Strasburg, third baseman Anthony Rendon, and left fielder Juan Soto, the Nationals won their first World Series in their 50-year history.

While in Canada, the team, then known as the Expos, developed outstanding talent—Rusty Staub, Tim Raines, Vladimir Guerrero, Andre Dawson, Larry Walker, Pedro Martinez, Moisés Alou, and Andrés Galarraga, as well as Hall of Fame catcher Gary Carter—but reaped little reward. The Expos' luck was so bad that when a players' strike closed down the major leagues in 1994, canceling the World Series, Montreal sported a 74-40 record, the best in baseball. The Expos' only playoff appearance occurred in 1981, another strike season, which was split in two. Montreal qualified for the playoffs by winning the second-half race, defeated the Phillies in five games, and then lost a heartbreaking five-game NLCS to the Dodgers.

Chicago Cubs

Founded in 1876
Other names: Chicago White Stockings, Chicago Colts, Chicago Orphans
3 World Championships (1907, 1908, 2016)
17 NL pennants

The Cubs were the best team in the National League in the first decade of the twentieth century, advancing to four World Series in a 5-year period, beating the Detroit Tigers in both 1907 and 1908 with a combined loss of only one game. They got back to the World Series in six more seasons, including 1945, when they fell to the Tigers in seven games and, apparently, suffered the Curse of the Billy Goat.

Stephen Strasburg

In recent years, young pitchers have been limited to a set number of innings in order to prevent arm injuries. However, the Washington Nationals set off a nationwide debate in 2012 when they announced that young star Stephen Strasburg would be limited to 160 innings, despite the team's involvement in a division race. Strasburg, who had a 15-6 record, made his final pitch of the season on September 8. Although the Nationals won their division without him, they faltered in their first playoff series without their ace.

According to legend, Billy Sianis, the owner of the Billy Goat Tavern in Chicago, brought his bar's mascot to the World Series at Wrigley Field. The goat was not permitted to enter because, he was told, it smelled. Sianis was so angry that he cursed the team, saying, "Them Cubs, they ain't gonna win no more!"

He was right. After losing that Series, the Cubs didn't even qualify for the playoffs for the next 38 years. They led, 3–0, in the deciding game of the 1984 NLCS before a ground ball went through an infielder's legs, and they lost to San Diego. What happened in 2003 was even worse. They held a 3–0 lead in the eighth inning of the game that could send them to the World Series, but some say a Cubs fan prevented Chicago left fielder Moisés Alou from catching a foul ball. Then the shortstop let a ground ball through his legs. The Cubs lost that game and the following game to the Marlins. However, after 108 years of misery for Cubs fans, the curse was finally broken in 2016 when the Cubs won a World Series behind young hitters like Kris Bryant, who also won the NL MVP award that year. Bryant and other key members of that championship team—Anthony Rizzo and Javier Báez—all were traded in midseason 2021 when the Cubs overhauled their roster.

fun fact

Wrigley Field

The Cubs started playing at Wrigley in 1916. Since then, Wrigley Field has become more than just a ballpark; it's a landmark in Chicago. The ivy-covered brick outfield walls, an old hand-operated scoreboard, and rooftop views from the surrounding apartment buildings all add to the unique atmosphere of the most popular park in the National League. Until 1988, all games at Wrigley were day games. Even now, the Cubs play more day games than any other team.

Famous Fungo!

Can you match the silly answers to the funny riddles?

1 What do you call a baseball player who only hits flapjacks?

2 What do you call a baseball player who throws dairy products?

3 What do you call a dog that stands behind home plate?

___ A milk pitcher!

___ A catcher's mutt!

___ A pancake batter!

Famous Cub: Ernie Banks, 1953–1971

HR	RBI	AVG
512	1,636	.274

Ernie Banks began his career in the Negro Leagues in 1950. He joined the Cubs as their shortstop in 1953. Banks was known for his deep love of the game, particularly where the Cubs were involved. It was Banks who first called Wrigley Field the "Friendly Confines," a nickname for the ballpark that's used regularly even today. In 1982, the Cubs retired Banks's number, 14—the first number they had ever retired. A bronze statue of Ernie Banks stands outside Wrigley Field in honor of the man called "Mr. Cub."

Chapter 4
The American League

The American League is sometimes called the "junior circuit," while the National League is the "senior circuit." Why? Because the AL was formed 25 years after the NL. Of course, the AL has still been around for as long as anyone can remember. It began in 1901 when the old Western League chose a new name and decided that they were just as much a major league as the National League.

There were eight teams in the original American League. All eight teams are still around, though only the Tigers are still in the same city with the same name.

The Original 1901 American League

1901 Team Name	Modern Team Name
Chicago White Stockings	Chicago White Sox
Boston Americans	Boston Red Sox
Detroit Tigers	Detroit Tigers
Philadelphia Athletics	Oakland Athletics
Baltimore Orioles	New York Yankees
Washington Senators	Minnesota Twins
Cleveland Blues	Cleveland Guardians
Milwaukee Brewers	Baltimore Orioles

Fifteen teams make up the American League today. The only major difference between an AL team and an NL team is the use of the designated hitter. Pitchers don't bat in games played in AL ballparks. The AL has enjoyed a significant advantage over the NL in this century, both in the results of the All-Star Game and interleague play. However, World Series success has been split almost evenly during the same period.

Kansas City Royals

Founded in 1969
2 World Championships (1985, 2015)
4 AL pennants

The Royals were one of baseball's best franchises in the 1980s. After three unsuccessful 1970s attempts to beat the Yankees in the AL playoffs, the team finally overcame New York to win the 1980 AL pennant, only to fall to the Phillies in the World Series. Dick Howser, fired by the Yankees for losing the 1980 ALCS, then led the Royals back to the World Series in 1985, and defeated Whitey Herzog's Cardinals in seven games. But then the Royals spent many years without success.

Professing the need to operate as a small-market team, they stayed in the bottom half of the league for two decades. Good thing they didn't trade left fielder Alex Gordon. In 2014, he led them to the playoffs as a wild card. They won the wild card game in extra innings, then won two extra-inning American League Division Series (ALDS) games against the Angels. The Royals swept the Orioles in the ALCS, and took the Giants to Game 7 in the World Series. One year later, the Royals won the World Series against the Mets. In each of the five games, the Mets took the lead, but in four games the Royals came back to win, including Games 1 and 5 in extra innings.

Famous Royal: George Brett, 1973–1993

HR	RBI	AVG
317	1,596	.305

George Brett spent his entire career with the Royals, and that career coincided with the best years of the Kansas City Royals franchise. He was a .300 hitter who also hit

fun fact

Waterfall in the Outfield

In 1973, the Royals moved into Royals Stadium, still one of the most beautiful major league parks. It was eventually renamed for long-time owner Ewing Kauffman. There aren't very many seats in the outfield at Kauffman Stadium. Instead, the Water Spectacular puts on a huge waterfall show between innings. A home run by the Royals can end up splashing!

15–20 home runs almost every year. As if that weren't good enough, he was even better in the postseason. In the 1978 ALCS, he hit 3 home runs in the same game.

Despite his awesome career, Brett might be best remembered for the "pine tar incident." In 1983, he hit a go-ahead home run against the Yankees, but he was called out for using an illegal bat that had too much sticky pine tar on it. Brett charged the umpire in a crazy, spitting rage. As it turned out, the commissioner later decided that the rule about pine tar on bats wasn't clear, so the home run counted. George Brett is the only Royal in the Hall of Fame. He was inducted in 1999.

Hink Pinks

Hink pinks are two rhyming words. Both words of each answer should have the same number of syllables. See if you can score four!

1. The heavier of two batters.

F _ _ _ _ _ B _ _ _ _ _

2. Where you throw a bad referee.

U _ _ D _ _ _ _

3. Nine baseball players shouting at once.

T _ _ _ S _ _ _ _ _

4. The last part of a baseball game when one team has more points.

W _ _ _ _ _ _ _ I _ _ _ _ _

Boston Red Sox

Founded in 1901
Other names: Boston Americans, Boston Pilgrims
9 World Championships (1903, 1912, 1915, 1916, 1918, 2004, 2007, 2013, 2018)
14 AL pennants

The Red Sox moved into Fenway Park in 1912 and won the World Series 4 of the next 7 years. Pitcher and all-time home run king Babe Ruth was the team's best player and a fan favorite. But in 1919, owner Harry Frazee traded Babe Ruth to the Yankees. Whether as a direct result of that mistake or not, the Red Sox didn't win another World Series for 86 years.

The Sox came close a few times during those years, only to lose in heartbreaking fashion. In 1975, they pushed the Reds to Game 7. In 1978, they lost a one-game playoff to the Yankees on a home run by Bucky Dent. In 1986, a ground ball through first baseman Bill Buckner's legs in the sixth game of the World Series allowed the Mets to score the winning run. In 2003, Yankee Aaron Boone eliminated the Sox with a walk-off home run in Game 7 of the ALCS. The Red Sox were cursed.

The curse seemed to be continuing at first in the 2004 postseason. The Yankees won the first three games of the ALCS—including a blistering 19–8 victory in Game 3. No team in the history of major league baseball had ever come back from a 3–0 deficit to win a seven-game series, but the Red Sox beat the odds and took the series. They went on to dispatch the Cardinals in four games to claim the World Championship. The Red Sox have continued to be a dominant power in the AL. They won another World Championship in 2007, and after bottoming out in 2012, they returned to the top of the baseball world in 2013 and again in 2018.

fun fact

Green Monster

Fenway Park is one of the majors' two ancient ballparks. To make the field fit inside the available space, Fenway's left field fence is very, very shallow—about 310 feet. So, to prevent a gazillion home runs to left field, the fence there is 37 feet high. Because the wall is so huge, and because it's painted green, it's called the "Green Monster."

Famous Red Sox: Ted Williams, 1939–1960

HR	RBI	AVG
521	1,839	.344

Ted Williams, known as "the Splendid Splinter," was one of the most remarkable hitters ever. He hit for power and a high average, and rarely ever struck out. In fact, after his career, he wrote a book called *The Science of Hitting*, which is still a terrific book to read for anyone who wants to learn to be a better hitter. As a rookie in 1939, Williams hit .327, and he batted .406 in 1941. No one has batted over .400 for an entire season since Williams did it—over 80 years ago! In 1942, Williams not only led the league in batting average again, but also led with 36 home runs and 137 runs batted in, winning the Triple Crown.

Williams's career was interrupted twice: once when he was drafted into the navy for World War II, and again when he volunteered to serve in the Korean War. Both times he returned to baseball to have great seasons. Williams finally called it quits at age 42 and was inducted into the Hall of Fame in 1966.

Texas Rangers

Founded in 1961
Other names: Washington Senators
0 World Championships
2 AL pennants

When the Washington Senators moved into a former minor-league ballpark in Arlington, Texas, in 1972, their only significant possessions were aged slugger Frank Howard and manager Ted Williams, one of the greatest hitters in baseball history. Howard was traded during the season and Williams resigned afterward. Their most notable accomplishments in the next 25 years were an ownership group that included a future Texas governor and the US president, George W. Bush, as well as the construction of a new ballpark in 1994.

Not until 1996 did the Rangers qualify for the playoffs, and they lost their first three postseason series, all to the Yankees, in 1996, 1998, and 1999. They reacted to a losing season in 2000 by signing Alex Rodriguez to a staggering 10-year $252 million contract. He was traded after three seasons in which his salary forced the Rangers to deplete their overall roster, particularly on the pitching side. They finally put together another playoff team after Ron Washington became manager and Hall of Fame pitcher Nolan Ryan rejoined the franchise as president.

Led by Most Valuable Player Josh Hamilton, infielder Michael Young, and rookie closer Neftalí Feliz, the Rangers reached the World Series in 2010. They enjoyed their best season the following year, when they returned to the World Series, and came within a strike of a World Championship in the ninth and tenth innings of Game 6, before being denied by the Cardinals. Feliz underwent surgery in 2012, after which Young was traded and Hamilton left as a free agent. Although the Rangers haven't qualified for the postseason since 2016, they did host the first neutral site World Series at their spanking new Globe Life Field in 2020.

words to know

no-hitter

When a pitcher allows no hits in a game. It's still a no-hitter if the pitcher walks batters or if batters reach base on fielding errors. In fact, it's possible for a pitcher to pitch a no-hitter but still lose the game.

Famous Ranger: Nolan Ryan, 1966–1993

W-L	ERA	K
324-292	3.19	5,714

Nolan Ryan was truly a flame-thrower, firing the ball harder and faster than anyone had ever seen. When Ryan came up with the Mets in 1966 he could throw very hard, but he had control problems and walked a lot of hitters. In 1972, the Mets traded him to the California Angels, and there he turned into a big winner and became the king of strikeouts. He led the league eleven times in strikeouts, and in 1973, he struck out a whopping 383 hitters. While most pitchers would be thrilled to throw one no-hitter in their careers, Ryan threw seven—a major league record.

A native of Texas, Ryan was excited when he got to play for the Houston Astros, where he topped Walter Johnson's long-held all-time career strikeout record in 1983 at the age of 36. Ryan, however, was far from done. Somehow, no matter how hard he threw, his arm never seemed to get tired. He surprised everyone by pitching in the big leagues for another 10 years, including several with the Rangers, until he finally retired at age 46. By that time he had over 5,000 strikeouts, far more than anyone else. He made the Hall of Fame in 1999—his Hall of Fame picture includes a Rangers cap.

New York Yankees

Founded in 1901
Other names: Baltimore Orioles, New York Highlanders
27 World Championships (1923, 1927, 1928, 1932, 1936, 1937, 1938, 1939, 1941, 1943, 1947, 1949, 1950, 1951, 1952, 1953, 1956, 1958, 1961, 1962, 1977, 1978, 1996, 1998, 1999, 2000, 2009)
40 AL pennants

The Yankees are the most successful major league team. They are the best-known team nationally, and even worldwide. They have been so good so often—since brewery owner Jacob Ruppert bought the club in 1915, and purchased the contract of Babe Ruth 5 years later—that it's easier to list the few times they *haven't* reached the postseason: 1965–74 and 1982–94 represent their longest times out of the playoffs since 1921. In their most recent dynasty, under manager Joe Torre, the Yankees won the World Series in 4 of 5 years between 1996 and 2000.

Although they reached the postseason eleven times in the next 12 years, some fans expressed disappointment with the Yankees, because they won only one World Series, in 2009, under Torre's successor, Joe Girardi. Yes, the Yankees have had expectations of a World Series victory every year since a partnership led by George Steinbrenner bought the franchise in 1973 from CBS. Known as "the Boss," Steinbrenner expanded the brand, raised the payroll to the largest in baseball, formed his own television network, and built a new Yankee Stadium before his death in 2010.

Many of the game's greatest players, starting with Ruth, have worn the Yankee pinstripes. Ruth teamed with Lou Gehrig to produce the first Yankee dynasty in the 1920s. Joe DiMaggio followed in the 1930s and 1940s, only to be replaced by Mickey Mantle in the 1950s. Roger Maris hit 61 home runs in 1961 to surpass Ruth's record of 60 in 1927. In the 1970s, Reggie Jackson became known as "Mr. October" for his postseason heroics. The great first baseman Don Mattingly joined the team in 1982, and retired in 1995 after only one playoff series, the last lean period in club history. Derek Jeter was the shortstop on five championship teams. Jeter, who retired after the 2014 season, is the best known and most loved of the recent Yankees.

Famous Yankee: Babe Ruth, 1914–1935

HR	RBI	AVG	W-L	ERA	K
714	2,213	.342	94-46	2.28	488

It's almost impossible to find anyone who hasn't heard of "the Babe." Also nicknamed "the Bambino," George Herman "Babe" Ruth could do it all. He began as a pitcher with the Boston Red Sox before moving to the outfield. He went on to change the face of baseball. When Ruth led the major leagues with 29 home runs in 1919, it was the first time a player had hit more than 25 in a season. He was traded to the Yankees, where he became the greatest home run hitter ever.

Baseball Diamond

Can you find six common baseball terms hidden in the diamond grid? Start at a letter and move one space at a time in any direction to a touching letter. You may not use the same letter twice in a word, but you can cross over your own path.

HINT: One of the terms is an abbreviation!

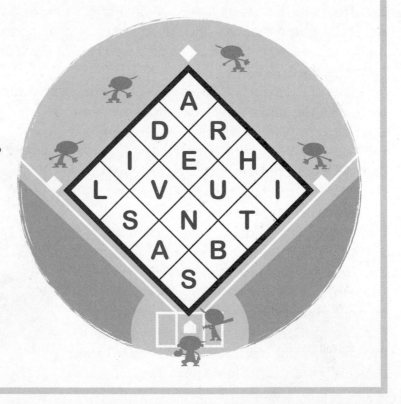

Ruth's 714 career home runs stood as the record until Hank Aaron passed that mark in 1974. Had Ruth not been a pitcher for several years, who knows how many he would have hit. He led the league in home runs (or tied for the lead) twelve times. He also batted .342 for his career and is still considered by most baseball historians as the greatest baseball player ever. Ruth led the Yankees to one World Series title after another. An often-told story says that in one World Series against the Cubs, Ruth stepped up to the plate, pointed to the bleachers where he was going to hit a home run...and then did just that.

Beyond baseball, Ruth was an enormously popular celebrity and was treated like royalty. The Babe enjoyed all the publicity and excitement that surrounded him. It was said that "as he moved, center stage moved with him." Ruth retired in 1935 and was one of the first five players elected to the Hall of Fame in 1936.

Famous Yankee: Lou Gehrig, 1923–1939

HR	RBI	AVG
493	1,995	.340

Gehrig was called "the Iron Horse" because he was always in the lineup. He batted right after the Babe in the great Yankees lineup and played in Ruth's shadow. Nonetheless, Gehrig was as awesome a hitter as anyone. For 14 consecutive years he drove in more than 100 runs, topping 170 three times and setting an American League record with 184 in 1931. He could do it all. He got more than 200 hits eight times, hit 40 home runs five times, and batted over .300 for 13 consecutive years. He hit 23 grand slam home runs, the most of all time until Alex Rodriguez hit his 24th in 2013.

Despite all of his amazing accomplishments, Gehrig is best known for two things: He began a streak in 1925 where he played every single game until 1939, or 2,130 consecutive games, a record most people thought would never be broken. (Cal Ripken Jr. has since topped that incredible record.) Unfortunately, the other thing Gehrig is best remembered for is the reason he removed himself from the lineup eight games into the 1939 season. Gehrig had been suffering from an unknown disease, which later became known as Lou Gehrig's disease. He retired from baseball in May 1939, and in July he famously described himself as the "luckiest man on the face of the earth" for the opportunity to have played for the Yankees, and to have been loved by the fans and by his wife. Less than 2 years later he died at the age of 37. He was elected into the Hall of Fame in 1939.

Tampa Bay Rays

Founded in 1998
Other names: Tampa Bay Devil Rays
0 World Championships
2 AL pennants

Despite one of the lowest payrolls in the major leagues, the Rays have enjoyed remarkable success since 2008, when they shot from last to first in the American League, facing the Phillies in the World Series. Hampered by an unloved domed stadium in sun-splashed St. Petersburg, Florida, and unable to attract large crowds, they nevertheless qualified for the playoffs on the last day of the season in both 2011 and 2013.

Joe Maddon, a former minor league catcher who spent decades with the Angels organization, maximized the talent of young players developed in the club's farm system after becoming the Rays' manager in 2006. His successor,

Pride of the Yankees

The movie *The Pride of the Yankees* is a marvelous, deeply touching story of Lou Gehrig's life.

Kevin Cash, has used a similar strategy. With the help of a remarkable offensive surge by Randy Arozarena, a rookie obtained in what appeared to be a minor trade with the Cardinals, the Rays advanced to the 2020 World Series which they lost to the Dodgers in six games. The Cuban-born Arozarena hit a record 10 home runs during the postseason and continued to shine in 2021 when the Rays led all AL teams with 100 victories.

Detroit Tigers

Founded in 901
4 World Championships (1935, 1945, 1968, 1984)
11 AL pennants

The opening of Comerica Park helped to revitalize decaying Detroit starting in 2000, but it wasn't until the arrival of manager Jim Leyland in 2006 that the Tigers emerged from the ruins. Under Leyland, the team enjoyed its first winning season in 13 years—a drought that included 119 losses in 2003—and the Tigers went all the way to the World Series before bowing to the Cardinals. Nine years later, led by Miguel Cabrera's Triple Crown hitting and Justin Verlander's power pitching, they returned to the World Series, only to suffer a sweep by the Giants. The Tigers' consecutive trips to the playoffs in 2011–2014 represent the best stretch for the team since the 1930s.

Detroit was among the more formidable teams during the early years of the AL, thanks mostly to the presence of Ty Cobb, perhaps the greatest hitter and most competitive player of his or any other era. In addition to Cobb, the Tigers have been represented by many Hall of Fame players, most notably Mickey Cochrane, Charlie Gehringer, Hank Greenberg, and Al Kaline.

fun fact

What's a Devil Ray, Anyway?

The Devil Rays were named after a strange sort of fish that looks more like a flying squirrel than a fish. In 2007, the team decided that they shouldn't be named after a fish. Now the "Rays" refer to rays of light.

Famous Tiger: Ty Cobb, 1905–1928

HR	RBI	AVG
117	1,938	.366

Cobb was one of the toughest players of all time. He worked very hard and spent hours practicing hitting, sliding, and throwing to make it to the major leagues in 1905 at the age of 18. The hard work paid off. Cobb played 24 years, almost all for the Tigers, and hit under .300 just once, as a rookie. He batted over .400 three times and led the league in batting average twelve times on his way to an incredible .366 career batting average. Cobb was also one of the best base stealers ever, stealing nearly 900 bases.

Cobb's hitting made him one of the first five players elected to the Hall of Fame in 1936. The fans enjoyed watching Cobb, but he rarely got along with his teammates, and opposing players hated him. He would sharpen his cleat spikes and then slide in hard, feet first. When his career was over, Cobb said that if he had one thing he could do differently it would be to have more friends.

Chicago White Sox

Founded in 1901
3 World Championships (1906, 1917, 2005)
6 AL pennants

Although the White Sox won a World Series in 2005, and Guaranteed Rate Field is the only modern ballpark in the city, they still trail the Chicago Cubs in popularity. Sometimes referred to as the "South Siders," because they play on the south side of the city, they traditionally finish second in

Manager Too

Cobb not only played for the Tigers; but for 6 years was a player-manager for them, too, amassing a 479-444 record. He took the Tigers as high as second place in the American League.

fun fact

Thirty-Game Winner

The last pitcher to top the 30-win mark was Denny McLain, who won thirty-one games for the Detroit Tigers in 1968. He's the only pitcher to win more than thirty games in a season in more than 50 years!

attendance to the Cubs and their ancient "shrine" of Wrigley Field on the prosperous north side.

The team was a powerhouse in the early years of the AL, but it led to the worst scandal in baseball history. In 1919, eight White Sox players were accused of conspiring with gamblers to lose the 1919 World Series to the Cincinnati Reds, and the group, which included the great hitter Shoeless Joe Jackson, was banned for life. The club didn't win another World Championship until 2005, although they did reach the 1959 World Series against the Los Angeles Dodgers, and won division titles in 1983, 1993, and 2000. After qualifying for the 2020 playoffs, the White Sox stunned the baseball world by luring Hall of Fame manager Tony La Russa out of retirement. La Russa, who started his managerial career in Chicago in 1980, was seventy-six and an old-school leader who appeared out of step with the current analytical approach to the game. Yet, behind solid starting pitching, the team opened a huge lead in the Central Division.

Los Angeles Angels

Founded in 1961
Other names: California Angels, Anaheim Angels, Los Angeles Angels of Anaheim
1 World Championship (2002)
1 AL pennant

For the first 35 years of their existence, the Angels—who shared Los Angeles with the Dodgers before moving to Anaheim in 1966—were owned by beloved cowboy star Gene Autry. He presided over only three playoff series, excruciating losses in the AL Championship Game, before his death. The Walt Disney Company was the beneficiary of the team's surge under manager Mike Scioscia in 2002, when the Angels rallied from a 5–0 deficit in Game 6 of the World Series, and defeated the Giants in Game 7 behind rookie pitchers John Lackey, Brendan Donnelly, and Frankie Rodriguez.

Big spending has characterized the attempts by owner Arte Moreno to establish the Angels as a contender in the AL West. His free-agent acquisitions included Vladimir Guerrero from the Expos, Albert Pujols, the three-time MVP with the Cardinals, and Josh Hamilton, the 2010 MVP with the Rangers. Yet, the Angels have managed to finish first in their division only once in the last 12 years.

But the owner's luck may have begun to change after the 2017 season. Moreno won a high-stakes battle for the rights to Shohei Ohtani, a 23-year-old who starred as a hitter and pitcher in Japan and insisted on doing both in the major leagues. The Rookie of the Year award he won in 2018 offered only a glimpse of the talent he would reveal in 2021 after two injury-plagued seasons. He became a dominant performer at the plate and on the mound and the number one attraction in baseball. The only disappointment was that his emergence happened at the same time as an injury to another Rookie of the Year, Mike Trout, limiting the team's effectiveness.

Famous Angel: Mike Trout, 2011–

HR	RBI	AVG
310	816	.305

At the beginning of his career, it seemed as if not even the Angels fully appreciated what they had in Mike Trout. Yes, they picked the New Jersey high school athlete in the first round of the 2009 draft but twenty-four players already were off the board. Not only was he the sixth outfielder chosen but the second by his own team, after Randal Grichuk.

Clever T-Shirt

When the Angels changed their name in 2005, deciding to call themselves the Los Angeles Angels of Anaheim, the Dodgers decided to have a bit of fun at the Angels' expense. They printed T-shirts that said "Los Angeles Dodgers of Los Angeles."

Yet, following his first full professional season, he was honored as the Minor League Player of the Year.

By the time he was 20, Trout was the starting center fielder for the Angels and the AL Rookie of the Year. His accomplishments are among the most remarkable in baseball history—nine all-star selections and eight Silver Slugger awards in his first nine seasons. Already he has earned three AL MVP titles and he never finished below the top five in MVP voting until 2021 when he suffered a severe calf injury in mid-May and could not play. The Angels were expecting Trout's return as the most complete player in the game in 2022.

Cleveland Guardians

Founded in 1901
Other names: Cleveland Blues, Cleveland Bronchos, Cleveland Naps, Cleveland Indians
2 World Championships (1920, 1948)
6 AL pennants

Of the eight original franchises still competing in the American League, none has waited longer for a World Championship than Cleveland. Not since 1948, when the owner was Bill Veeck; the manager was Lou Boudreau, a Hall of Fame shortstop; and the home park was cavernous Municipal Stadium, has the team won a Series. So consistently bad were the teams during much of the 1970s and 1980s that they inspired a movie about unwanted castoffs called *Major League*.

However, the team became perennial contenders in the 1990s by signing talented young players to long-term contracts financed in part by the move to a beautiful, intimate ballpark, Jacobs Field (now Progressive Field). From 1995 through 2001, Cleveland advanced to the playoffs six times and reached the World Series in 1995 and 1997. After a seven-game loss to the

Red Sox in the 2007 ALCS, they fell out of contention until 2013, when former Boston manager Terry Francona guided a largely anonymous roster to an unexpected wild card berth. In the 2016 World Series, they forced a seventh game, pushing the Cubs to extra innings but ultimately losing.

Famous Indian: Bob Feller, 1936–1956

W-L	ERA	K
266-162	3.25	2,581

Feller was the dominant American League pitcher in the years around World War II. His background as an Iowa farmer made him a strong teenager and propelled him to the majors at a young age. He struck out seventeen batters in a game when he was only 17 years old, and he had won twenty major league games when he was still 20 years old. Feller's career was interrupted by 4 years of service in the navy during the war. He returned to the field in the late 1940s and continued pitching until 1956. He claims to have thrown faster fastballs than Nolan Ryan. Feller was sometimes unhittable, but he walked more batters than anyone else too. He was elected to the Hall of Fame in 1962 in his first ballot.

Toronto Blue Jays

Founded in 1977
2 World Championships (1992, 1993)
2 AL pennants

Not only is it the most famous moment of club history; it also doubles as the most famous baseball moment in the history of Canada. Although the Blue Jays are the second major league franchise to play north of the US border—following

---

fun fact

A New Name

As of the 2022 season, the Cleveland team, one of the eight original teams still competing in the American League, is no longer known as the Indians. The name "Guardians" comes from the Guardians of Traffic, eight large statues on the Hope Memorial Bridge near Progressive Field. They now stand guard over a club that has waited longer for a championship than any other in baseball.

the Montreal Expos—they are the only one to win a World Series. They won two in a row and their second, in 1993, was particularly memorable. Joe Carter's 3-run homer in the ninth inning of Game 6 against the Phillies was just the second time that a World Series was determined by a walk-off homer.

It marked the culmination of the Blue Jays' rise from humble beginnings as an expansion team in 1977, playing in cold Exhibition Stadium, to the modernistic SkyDome (now Rogers Centre), with its retractable roof and center field hotel. The team had eleven straight winning seasons and five trips to the playoffs in the 1980s and 1990s.

Vladimir Guerrero Jr. and a host of young offensive talent have boosted the Blue Jays back into contention despite logistical problems unique to the team during the COVID-19 pandemic. Not only were they prevented from playing at their home park, but they were banned from their home country because the border between the US and Canada was closed to nonessential travel.

After riding out the 2020 season at a minor league facility in Buffalo, New York, the Blue Jays began the 2021 campaign at their spring-training site in Florida, before spending the next two months in Buffalo. They finally were allowed back in Canada, with modified attendance, in July 2021 and responded with an energetic and welcome push that fell one game short of a wild card berth.

fun fact

Sellout Streak

From 1995 until 2001, every seat at Jacobs Field was sold out every night for 455 games in a row. Afterward, the Cleveland team retired the number 455 in honor of their fans.

Minnesota Twins

Founded in 1901
Other names: Washington Senators, Washington Nationals
3 World Championships (1924, 1987, 1991)
6 AL pennants

The Washington Senators were one of the AL's original eight teams. In 1961, the Senators moved to the twin cities of Minneapolis–St. Paul, Minnesota, and became the Twins. The team originally played in cold Metropolitan Stadium but moved indoors to the Metrodome in 1982.

The Metrodome helped the team win their first World Series in Minnesota. In 1987, the Twins had the best home record in the league (56-21), but on the road they were 33-52. In the playoffs and the World Series they won every game in the Metrodome. Similarly, in 1991, the Twins beat the Braves 4–3 in the World Series, winning all four games in the Metrodome. The Twins moved to outdoor Target Field in 2010 and won 101 games as recently as 2019 but have failed to advance beyond the first round of the playoffs.

Famous Twin: Kirby Puckett, 1984–1995

HR	RBI	AVG
207	1,085	.318

Though he was only 5'8", Kirby Puckett played baseball like a giant. His batting average was .288 in his *worst* season. He also hit for power, hitting double-digit home runs in nine of his twelve seasons. In addition to his batting skills, Puckett was known as an outstanding defensive outfielder. Highlights of his playing days show him crashing into the Metrodome's "Hefty Bag" outfield wall, making catch after spectacular catch. The highlight of Puckett's career came in the 1991 World Series. In Game 6, he drove in a run with a triple, he made an amazing catch in front of the left center field wall, and he won the game with a walk-off home run in the eleventh inning.

In 1995, Puckett was hit in the head by a pitch, which broke his jaw. Puckett developed eye problems and never

fun fact

O, Canada!

Baseball games traditionally begin with the singing of the US national anthem, "The Star-Spangled Banner." But if the Blue Jays are in town, you'll also hear the Canadian anthem, "O Canada."

played a major league game again. He became one of the youngest Hall of Famers ever when he was elected on the first ballot in 2001.

Oakland Athletics

Founded in 1901
Other names: Philadelphia Athletics, Kansas City Athletics
9 World Championships (1910, 1911, 1913, 1929, 1930, 1972, 1973, 1974, 1989)
15 AL pennants

The Athletics, frequently shortened to A's by both fans and the media, were the brainchild of one man. Connie Mack, a former catcher, served as manager, part owner, and conscience of the club during its first 50 years of existence, all in Philadelphia. He developed many great players—among them Eddie Collins, Lefty Grove, Al Simmons, and Jimmie Foxx—and fielded several great teams, earning eight pennants and five World Championships, but he couldn't afford to retain the talent.

When the A's were sold to investors from Kansas City in 1955, they were a last-place team, and stayed near the bottom of the AL throughout their thirteen seasons in the Midwest. Enter Charles O. Finley, an insurance man from Indiana, who bought the team, dressed it in gaudy gold and green uniforms, and moved it to a new stadium in Oakland. He also signed a lot of good young players. Reggie Jackson, Catfish Hunter, Joe Rudi, Sal Bando, and Rollie Fingers became the nucleus of the great A's teams that won the World Series in 1972, 1973, and 1974, the only franchise other than the Yankees to win three consecutive championships.

In the post-Finley era, the "Bash Brothers," Mark McGwire and Jose Canseco, led the team to three consecutive World

Series appearances, but they won only once: the 1989 classic that was interrupted by the San Francisco Bay earthquake. In 1997, amid a dropoff in talent and falling attendance, the A's hired Billy Beane as general manager. Using an approach known as "moneyball," he resurrected the team without spending a lot of money. Oakland qualified for the playoffs five times in the decade starting in 2000 and, after a few years of mediocrity, advanced to the postseason on six occasions in the 2010s.

Famous Athletic: Rickey Henderson, 1979–2003

HR	RBI	AVG
297	1,115	.279

Rickey Henderson was fast. He had a lot of other great qualities, but the one thing that really defined him as a ballplayer was his outstanding speed. He stole more than one hundred bases in three separate seasons, including an amazing 130 in 1982! He led the league in stolen bases twelve times, including nine times in his first eleven seasons. At the plate, Henderson was a great all-around hitter. He had a great eye for the strike zone, leading the league in walks four times. He could hit for average, focusing on singles to get on base, or for power—extra-base hits and home runs—and he simply had a knack for getting on base. He won the AL MVP award in 1990 after he hit .325 with 28 home runs and had a league-leading sixty-five stolen bases as well as a league-leading on-base percentage of .439. He won the World Series twice, and was elected to the Hall of Fame in 2009 on the first ballot, with about 95 percent of the voters choosing to enshrine him.

Baltimore Orioles

Founded in 1901
Other names: Milwaukee Brewers, St. Louis Browns
3 World Championships (1966, 1970, 1983)
7 AL pennants

The Orioles were mostly failures during their 52-year existence as the St. Louis Browns, qualifying for their only World Series in the war year of 1944, against the Cardinals, with whom they shared a ballpark. Unable to compete against the Cardinals for the support of the community, they moved to Baltimore in 1954. It wasn't until 1960 that the talent was sufficient enough to form a contender, and a trade for Frank Robinson pushed them over the top in 1966, when the slugger won a Triple Crown in batting. Robinson remained a key figure as the Orioles won three successive pennants and a second World Series in 1970. The arrival of iron man Cal Ripken drove them to their most recent Series win in 1983 but their major legacy is Oriole Park at Camden Yards, whose design set the standard for new baseball parks.

After a 14-year drought under six different managers, the Orioles finally posted a winning season and reached the playoffs in 2012. Buck Showalter led the franchise back to prominence with the help of a home run surge keyed by the emergence of Chris Davis, an outstanding bullpen, and an unprecedented 29-9 record in games decided by one run. The relatively young team restored the pride established by the great Baltimore clubs managed by the late Earl Weaver in the late 1960s and early 1970s.

Famous Oriole: Cal Ripken Jr., 1981–2001

HR	RBI	AVG
431	1,695	.276

Cal Ripken Jr. was named Rookie of the Year in 1982 and MVP in 1983 and 1991. He established himself as one of the top players in modern baseball. Ripken always came to play—and play hard—day in and day out. In late 1995, he went from a star to a legend when he broke a record that most thought could never be topped—Ripken played in his 2,131st consecutive game, breaking the Iron Horse record set by the great Lou Gehrig. Ripken played 501 more consecutive games before taking himself out of the lineup in September 1998.

During the 2001 season, Ripken announced his retirement after 20 years with the Orioles. He was inducted into the Hall of Fame in 2007. In his career, Ripken played in 3,001 games and had 3,184 hits, 431 home runs, and nearly 1,700 RBIs. He was also one of the best-liked and most respected individuals who ever played in the major leagues.

Seattle Mariners

Founded in 1977
0 World Championships
0 AL pennants

Although this expansion club had a losing record in each of its first 14 years, it holds the American League standard for most victories in a regular season, 116, set in 2001. That happened to be the first year in US baseball for Ichiro Suzuki, a legendary hitter from Japan, and the next-to-last year in Seattle for manager Lou Piniella, who led the Mariners to their only four playoff appearances.

Under Piniella, the team enjoyed its first moment of success when the Mariners defeated the Angels in a one-game elimination for the 1995 AL West title, then rallied to defeat the Yankees in a thrilling division series. The victory, completed at the dreary Kingdome, was credited with ensuring the vote for the construction of Safeco Field, even though the Mariners subsequently lost to Cleveland in the ALCS. The club continued to win in ensuing years, despite the defections of such stars as Tino Martinez, Randy Johnson, Ken Griffey Jr., and Alex Rodriguez. None were with the team in 2001 when Suzuki, who earned both the Rookie of the Year and MVP awards, helped the team tie the record win total of the 1906 Cubs. Alas, they fell short against the Yankees in the ALCS and have not returned to the playoffs.

Famous Mariner: Ken Griffey Jr., 1989–2010

HR	RBI	AVG
630	1,836	.284

For a long time, people just called him "Junior," because his dad was also named Ken Griffey and was a great player for the Reds. In fact, when Griffey joined the majors in 1989, he played on the Seattle Mariners alongside his dad—the first time that had ever happened. Griffey, who genuinely loved to play the game, was one of the greatest center fielders ever, making many amazing catches and winning the Gold Glove for defense 10 years in a row. He was a major home run threat as well, often compared to the great Willie Mays. Griffey hit 56 home runs in 1997 and again in 1998, and he had more than 140 RBIs each year. In 2000, he joined the Cincinnati Reds, the team on which his dad became famous. Unfortunately, injury after injury slowed Junior down. Griffey hit his 500th home run in 2004, and his career total of 630

> ## fun fact
>
> ### The Mariner Moose
>
> In 1990, the Mariners chose the Moose as their official mascot. He appears at all home games, as well as on television ads and at community events. The Mariner Moose has earned fame for his recklessness. He broke his ankle when he crashed into the outfield wall on roller skates, and he nearly ran down one of the Red Sox on his cart.

ranks seventh on the all-time home run list. Seattle acquired Junior from the Reds in 2009 so that he could finish his career on the team with which he is most identified.

Houston Astros

Founded in 1962
Other names: Houston Colt .45s
1 World Championship (2017)
1 NL pennant; 3 AL pennants

The Astros, originally known as the Colt .45s, became an NL expansion team in 1962, and took their new name after moving into baseball's first domed stadium, the Astrodome, in 1965. They didn't have any sustained success until the 1980s, when they made three playoff appearances, and lost the 1986 NLCS to the Mets in an epic Game 6 settled in the sixteenth inning. Nineteen years later, during their sixth playoff trip in a 9-year period that featured the Killer B's—Jeff Bagwell, Craig Biggio, and Lance Berkman—the Astros defeated the Braves in eighteen innings to clinch an NL division series, then lost Game 3 of their first ever World Series, a sweep by the White Sox, in fourteen innings.

In 2013, the Astros switched leagues, going from the NL Central division to the AL West division. They continued their long history of bad play for a few years while some of their young players developed their skills. They made the playoffs in 2015 and then won the World Series for the first time in franchise history in 2017 with the help of that year's AL MVP José Altuve.

People, particularly their rivals, still are talking about that 2017 season. That's not necessarily a good thing: Major league baseball confirmed in early 2020 that the team used a camera

What kind of baseball players practice in the Arctic Circle?

Color in each box with a dot in the upper right-hand corner to find the silly answer to this riddle.

I wonder if they pitch snowballs?

system to steal signs during the 2017 season and postseason as well as part of 2018. In other words, the Astros cheated.

Although it cost the manager and general manager their jobs, the Houston players suffered no more than public harassment, particularly in New York and Los Angeles. And they have managed to deal with the fallout quite well, qualifying for the playoffs the next five seasons and advancing to the World Series in both 2019 and 2021 before losing to the Nationals and Braves, respectively.

Famous Astro: Craig Biggio, 1988–2007

HR	RBI	AVG
291	1,175	.281

Craig Biggio joined the Astros in 1988 as the rare catcher who could hit well, and he made the all-star team in 1991 as a catcher. Biggio moved to second base in 1992—and made the all-star team again.

Biggio has played in more games than any other Astro. At his last game in 2007, a sold-out crowd cheered him into retirement. The Astros retired his number, 7, the next year. Though he's from New York, 20 years of playing in Houston seem to have rubbed off on Biggio, who coached his sons' high school baseball teams while serving as assistant to the general manager of the Astros. He was inducted into the Hall of Fame in 2015.

One of the great things about baseball is that on any given day anyone can be the big hero. It's fun to hear about people like Bucky Dent or Francisco Cabrera, who were never stars but happened to get a hit at an incredibly important time. But the best baseball players are the hitters who get important hits every couple of games and the pitchers who are so good so often that no one wants to hit against them. These are today's stars who could be tomorrow's Hall of Famers.

Premier Pitchers

Forty years ago, a starting pitcher was expected to pitch eight or nine innings. Nowadays, relief pitchers are used a lot more, and even reliable starters often pitch only five or six innings. That hasn't changed the fact that the most important player a team can have is an "ace" starter, someone you can rely on to shut down an opponent every time he takes the mound. Here are the best of the major league aces, with stats updated through the 2021 season.

Jacob deGrom

W	ERA	K
77	2.50	1,505

Jacob deGrom goes to show that wins aren't always the best way to judge a pitcher. He's never led the league in wins and the most he's ever had in a season is 15. But that's not because he's a bad pitcher. Every time he's on the mound, he gives his team a chance to win—but his offense often doesn't score enough runs to do so. He strikes out a lot of batters and doesn't allow many base runners, leading the National League in strikeouts in 2019.

No one in modern history enjoyed such a spectacular start as deGrom did in 2021, when he managed a 0.56 earned run average in his first ten games. After fifteen appearances on the mound, his ERA (1.08) drew favorable comparisons to Bob Gibson's astonishing 1.12 in 1968. But arm injuries sidelined him in early July and the Mets can only hope he returns as the best starting pitcher in baseball.

Walker Buehler

W	ERA	K
40	2.90	632

words to know

save

When a pitcher comes into a close ballgame and gets the final outs.

Although the Dodgers listed four Cy Young Award recipients on their roster during the 2021 season, the leader who emerged wasn't one of them. Walker Buehler, whose accomplishments include a College World Series and professional World Series championship by the time he was 26, has become the most consistent and dependable pitcher on the staff. In winning twelve of his first fourteen decisions in 2021, Buehler allowed only one earned run in each of his first two defeats.

Max Scherzer

W	ERA	K
190	3.16	3,020

Max Scherzer grew up near St. Louis. When he finished high school, his hometown Cardinals drafted him. But Scherzer chose to attend college at the University of Missouri instead of turning pro. Four years later, he joined the Diamondbacks organization, earning a promotion to the majors in 2008. He was traded to the Tigers in 2010, and to the Dodgers in 2021.

fun fact

Time to Rotate the Pitchers!

A starting pitcher can't pitch every day—his arm would get too sore. Since games are scheduled almost every day, teams usually use a rotation of five pitchers who take turns starting.

fun fact

Hard to Replace

Wins above replacement (WAR) is an advanced statistic that tries to show how important a player is to his team. Although he was only a rookie in 2012, Mike Trout's WAR was 10.9, the highest number since Barry Bonds's 11.8 in 2002. That means if the Angels hadn't had Trout, the team would have had more than ten fewer wins, and it explains why he finished second in voting for the AL MVP award to Triple Crown winner Miguel Cabrera. Even for the best players, a WAR above 7.0 is outstanding.

Throughout his early career, Scherzer impressed scouts with his strikeout rate, which in 2012 was the best in all of baseball. The next year, Scherzer won the Cy Young Award while allowing the fewest base runners per game of any pitcher in the majors.

Scherzer continued his all-star-level performance, winning a World Series after moving to the Washington Nationals. He threw two no-hitters in the same year in 2015 and then won the Cy Young Award twice more, in 2016 and 2018, leading the league in strikeouts both years. With the Dodgers, Scherzer continues his advance toward the Hall of Fame.

Gerrit Cole

W	ERA	K
117	3.20	1,673

He was challenged for his ability to spin a baseball. He was knocked out temporarily by the COVID-19 virus. But Gerrit Cole ultimately prevailed in lifting the Yankees into a playoff race they almost abandoned in the first half of the 2021 season. Although allegations about his doctoring a baseball led to umpires examining all pitchers as they left the mound and he endured a fifteen-day COVID layoff, he responded with some brilliant performances that justified his contract as the highest-paid pitcher in the major leagues.

Other Starting Pitchers

Lance Lynn is a burly, bearded right-hander anchoring the staff of his fifth major league team, the White Sox. Lynn received all-star recognition and was among the AL's leaders in ERA while setting the standard for a team managed by Tony La Russa, his first manager with the Cardinals in his debut season of 2011. An experienced right-hander who drew little attention in five solid seasons with the Mets, Zack Wheeler has been a godsend for the Phillies. He led the entire NL in innings pitched, strikeouts, and wins above replacement for much of the 2021 season. Of the three young starters for the upstart Brewers, Corbin Burnes was the strikeout king, tying a mark set by Hall of Famer Tom Seaver by fanning ten consecutive batters in a game, and establishing a record of his own by striking out fifty-eight batters before issuing his first walk of the 2021 season. At 27, he's just beginning to dazzle.

Top Hitters

Vladimir Guerrero Jr.

HR	RBI	AVG
72	213	.289

In 2019, approximately nine months after his father accepted his Hall of Fame plaque in Cooperstown, New York, Vladimir Guerrero Jr. stepped into the batter's box for Toronto and another generation of major league pitchers got very nervous. Only 20, Junior was slightly shorter and considerably heavier than his dad but the hand-eye coordination was frighteningly similar. Two years later, after shedding 42 pounds, the younger Guerrero became an offensive star, challenging in all three categories of the Triple Crown and earning the All-Star Game MVP award after a monstrous home run which he dedicated to his father.

Game Pieces

Baseball is such a familiar game that you might not even need words to describe it! Study the four picture puzzles below and see if you can figure out what baseball play, player, or place they each describe.

MVP

The abbreviation for "Most Valuable Player." One player in each league wins the MVP award every year, not only for being a great player, but usually for helping their team get to the playoffs. The Baseball Writers' Association of America chooses who wins the MVP award.

Fernando Tatis Jr.

HR	RBI	AVG
81	195	.292

Another son of a Dominican baseball player, Fernando Tatis Jr. also reached the major leagues in 2019 and achieved true stardom at age 22. This Junior is an energetic shortstop whose presence has transformed the Padres into a playoff contender. He plays with such reckless abandon that he suffered a partial dislocation of his left shoulder three times in 2021 and came back as good as ever. On the third occasion, after the team endured a four-game losing streak in mid-August, he returned (as an outfielder) to hit 2 homers and drive in 4 runs in an essential victory.

Ronald Acuna Jr.

HR	RBI	AVG
105	246	.281

At the time of his knee injury at midseason in 2021, Ronald Acuna Jr. was leading all major league players with 72 runs scored. That was just one of the indicators that enable his supporters to claim the Braves outfielder may be the best all-around player in baseball. Two others: The Venezuela native hit a combined 55 home runs while stealing forty-five bases in 2019 and the shortened season of 2020. The former NL Rookie of the Year is in the midst of a contract that ties him to Atlanta for most of the decade.

Silver Slugger award

An award for excellence given every year to the best hitter at each position in both the National and American League.

Other Great Hitters

Still young enough to be considered a prodigy, Juan Soto has become the face of the Washington team and an outfielder around whom the Nationals are planning to rebuild. A hero in the team's surprise march to a championship in 2019, he burnished his credentials with an NL batting title in 2020 and a triumph over Shohei Ohtani in the first round of the 2021 Home Run Derby. Yes, he's that good.

There should be a special place for highly successful longtime players for one team, notably José Abreu and Freddie Freeman. The first basemen not only won the MVP awards in their respective leagues in 2020 but they continued to make headlines in 2021, the eighth season for Abreu in Chicago and the eleventh full-time season for Freeman in Atlanta. Consider that both have averaged in the vicinity of 100 runs batted in per 162 games. No position has demonstrated more offensive potential than shortstop. In addition to Fernando Tatis Jr, other standouts include Brandon Crawford of the Giants, Xander Bogaerts of the Red Sox, and Tim Anderson of the White Sox. And the Dodgers, who seem to have more of everything, added second all-star Trea Turner in a trade despite the presence of the accomplished Corey Seager.

> ### ⚾ fun fact
>
> ### Classic Game
>
> For more than 40 years, *Strat-O-Matic* (www.strat-o-matic.com) has been making the ideal baseball board game. You can select your favorite team from the past season or pick up some classic teams from years gone by. There is a computerized version, but the standard version with cards and dice is still as wonderful as ever.

Double Duty

Shohei Ohtani

W	ERA	K
13	3.53	222
HR	**RBI**	**AVG**
93	247	.264

Not satisfied with being among baseball's home run leaders in 2021, the Japanese-born Ohtani became one of the AL's best starting pitchers. The first player in a century to succeed at both and the first to even attempt the double in the same season, he was the centerpiece of the 2021 All-Star Game, in which he started on the mound and batted leadoff. There appears to be no limit to what the Angels' superstar can achieve.

The Baseball Hall of Fame

In 1936, the baseball community decided that they needed a place to honor the greatest players ever. In June 1939, the National Baseball Hall of Fame and Museum was opened in Cooperstown, New York. It's a place where you'll find bats and gloves used by the greatest players, balls that were hit for historic home runs, and plenty of other neat baseball stuff. The Hall features plaques honoring the 333 members, which include 263 former major league players along with managers and other people closely associated with the game. There are even some umpires included.

How to Make It Into the Hall of Fame

Making the Hall of Fame is a tremendous honor that only a small number of baseball players ever receive. A player must be retired from baseball for 5 years before he is eligible to be elected to the Hall. Most players are voted in by baseball writers—writers can vote for up to ten players on each year's ballot. A player who receives votes from three-fourths of the writers gets inducted into the Hall of Fame. Generally, only two to five players make the Hall of Fame each year.

There is a lot to see at the Hall, including films and even an actual ball field where two major league teams square off every summer in a special exhibition game. The Hall of Fame also has special programs that include movies and "sandlot stories" about the game. There are also book

How do you get to the Baseball Hall of Fame?

To find the answer, follow the correct path from PLAY BALL to GAME OVER. Collect the letters along the way, and write them in order on the lines below.

_____ , _____ , _____ !

signings by some of the many authors—including former players, managers, and popular broadcasters—who write about the game. There's even a daily scavenger hunt for kids to take part in during the summer months. You may have to move through the Hall of Fame slowly because it's crowded, and there's so much to check out!

A Little History of the Hall

The idea for the Hall of Fame began in Cooperstown in the 1930s. Cooperstown was where Abner Doubleday, whom many credit with inventing the game, had lived, so it seemed to be the ideal place to build a museum to honor the game. In 1936, as baseball approached its 100th anniversary, plans were made to honor the greatest players of the game. That year, five players—Ty Cobb, Babe Ruth, Honus Wagner, Christy Mathewson, and Walter Johnson—were voted in as the first players to make the Hall of Fame.

By 1939, the actual building was completed. There was a big ceremony that summer, and the Hall of Fame was officially opened, displaying all sorts of stuff from the game. It was a small museum at first, but thousands of people flocked to tiny Cooperstown to visit. Over the years the Hall has grown, with new wings added on to accommodate all of the new exhibits plus a gallery, a library, and more. Today, between 300,000 and 400,000 people visit the baseball shrine annually. That's quite a lot of visitors for a town whose population is only 1,700 people.

Chapter 6
The World Series

A Treasury of World Series Information

The *Baseball Almanac* website, www.baseball-almanac.com, includes detailed summaries of every World Series, including box scores from each game.

fun fact

Subway Series

In New York City, most people get from place to place via the subway. When two New York teams play each other in the World Series, it's called a "Subway Series." The most recent Subway Series was in 2000, when the Yankees beat the Mets.

"The Fall Classic," as the World Series is often called, is the peak of the baseball season, when the best in the American League and the best in the National League square off for the championship of major-league baseball. Many of baseball's greatest players have performed at their best, and many of baseball's most memorable moments have occurred during the World Series.

Origins of the World Series

The World Series began in 1903, when representatives of the National League and the American League agreed to a competition that determined an overall champion. In a system that lasted through 1968, the team that won the most games in each league during the season won the pennant and the two pennant winners met in the World Series. The only play-off games required were to break ties for first place. But when the leagues expanded from ten to twelve teams in 1969, they were divided into two divisions of six teams each. The top teams in each division participated in a playoff series, with the winners reaching the World Series. Now there are thirty major league teams and three divisions in each league, plus three rounds of playoffs. But no matter how they get there, the survivors in each league compete in the World Series.

The Yankees have appeared in more World Series and won more championships than any other team. Between 1921 and 1964, the Yankees qualified for the World Series twenty-nine times. Fittingly, they won the championship four times in the last 5 years of the twentieth century, for an overall total of twenty-seven titles.

Over a Century of the World Series

Many of baseball's most memorable moments occurred in World Series games. Here are some highlights of notable World Series events.

1903: The first World Series pitted the Pittsburgh Pirates against the Boston Americans, who were renamed the Red Sox 5 years later. The Americans won the Series, which began on September 16, five games to three; Cy Young won two games for Boston.

1904: Manager John McGraw refused to allow his New York Giants, the NL champions, to play the AL champion Boston Americans because he said the American League was inferior. It was the first of only 2 years in which there was no World Series.

1905: The New York Giants defeated the Philadelphia Athletics, four games to one, with every game ending in a shutout. Giants star Christy Mathewson threw three complete-game shutouts and walked only one batter in the most amazing pitching performance in World Series history.

1908: The Chicago Cubs beat the Detroit Tigers, four games to one, to win their second championship in as many years. They then waited 108 years for their next one.

1918: Babe Ruth was the winning pitcher in two games as the Boston Red Sox claimed their third World Series victory in 4 years, beating the Chicago Cubs four games to two. The Red Sox failed to win another World Series for 86 years.

1919: The Chicago White Sox were denounced as the Black Sox after they were accused of deliberately losing the World Series to the Cincinnati Reds, five games to three, because they were paid money by gamblers. Eight White Sox players, including great hitter Joe Jackson, were banned for life from professional baseball, and the franchise didn't win another World Series until 2005.

Best of Seven

The World Series is played as a best-of-seven series: This means that the first team to win four games wins the Series, and there can't be more than seven games. In 1903, and again in 1919 through 1921, the Series was played as a best of nine. It returned to a best-of-seven format in 1922 and has remained so ever since.

Perfect Game

A pitcher pitches a perfect game when he retires all twenty-seven consecutive batters in a game. That's happened twenty-three times in the major leagues since 1900, including once in a World Series.

Lots of Games

Catcher Yogi Berra of the Yankees played seventy-five World Series games—more than anyone else ever has.

1936: The Yankees scored 18 runs in Game 2 and 13 runs in Game 6 on the way to a 4–2 World Series win against their Manhattan-based rivals, the Giants. It was the Yankees' first World Series without Ruth and featured Lou Gehrig and Joe DiMaggio together for the first time in the postseason.

1954: In the first game of the Series between the New York Giants and the Cleveland Indians, Willie Mays made what many consider baseball's most famous catch, running to the deepest part of center field at the Polo Grounds and snaring a Vic Wertz drive with his back to home plate to keep the score tied. The Giants went on to win that game and the next three over the favored Indians for a four-game sweep.

1956: Journeyman Don Larsen of the Yankees pitched the only perfect game in World Series history in Game 5, and his team defeated the Brooklyn Dodgers one last time in seven games. The Dodgers moved to Los Angeles after the 1957 season.

1960: Second baseman Bill Mazeroski hit the first World Series–winning walk-off home run in history in the ninth inning of Game 7, lifting the Pirates to a championship over the mighty Yankees despite being outscored 55–27.

1966: An amazing Baltimore Orioles pitching staff shut out the Los Angeles Dodgers in the final three games of a four-game sweep. The Dodgers scored only 2 runs and collected a total of seventeen hits, batting an anemic .142.

1969: Known as the worst team in baseball over the first 7 years of their existence, the New York Mets stunned the baseball world by winning one hundred games in the regular season, then beating the favored Orioles four games to one. Game 3 featured two amazing catches by Mets center fielder Tommie Agee.

1975: It's a classic instance of baseball drama, one that has been replayed on television year after year: Carlton Fisk attempted to wave his drive fair. The Hall of Fame catcher

The "Whole World" Series

While the World Series is played in America, baseball is popular all over the world! See if you can match the country names with their location to fill in the grid. We left you the W-O-R-L-D S-E-R-I-E-S to help.

TOGO   MEXICO
PERU   ITALY
EGYPT   TAIWAN
IRAN   CANADA
COOK ISLANDS
PUERTO RICO
RUSSIA

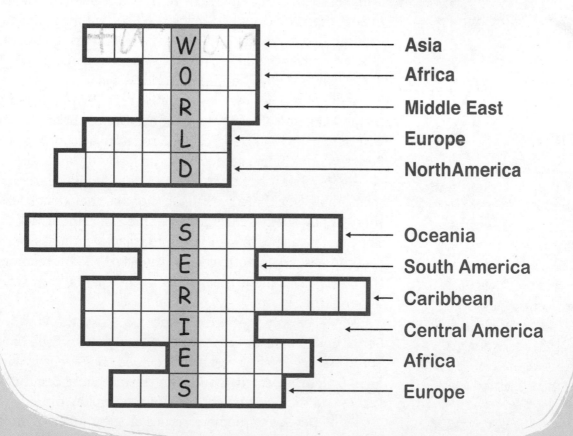

Asia

Africa

Middle East

Europe

NorthAmerica

Oceania

South America

Caribbean

Central America

Africa

Europe

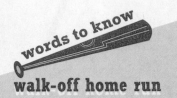

words to know

walk-off home run

A home run that is hit in the bottom of the ninth inning or in the bottom of an extra inning that wins the game. Following the home run, the teams walk off the field. The game is over, regardless of how many outs are left, because the opposing team won't have a chance to score.

fun fact

Bucky Dent

The Yankees and the Red Sox ended the 1978 season tied for first place in the American League East. They played one game to decide which team went to the playoffs. The Yankees shortstop, Bucky Dent, hit only 5 home runs all season. But he hit the biggest homer of his career to win the game for the Yankees and extend the Curse of the Bambino.

staved off elimination for the Red Sox in Game 6 with a twelfth-inning homer over Fenway Park's Green Monster. However, after falling behind early, the Cincinnati Reds rallied in Game 7 to win a thrilling World Series in which 1 run decided five games.

1977: Reggie Jackson, a member of three championship teams with the Oakland A's earlier in the decade, hit 3 consecutive home runs for the Yankees in a deciding Game 6 against the Los Angeles Dodgers. The slugger hit 5 homers and batted .450 in the Series, adding to his reputation as "Mr. October."

1986: Down to their final out in the tenth inning of Game 6, the Mets completed a remarkable 3-run comeback to beat the Red Sox, when Mookie Wilson hit a ground ball through first baseman Bill Buckner's legs, scoring Ray Knight to force a seventh game. The Mets also overcame a 3–0 deficit to win Game 7 and the World Series.

1988: A gimpy Kirk Gibson pinch-hit a 2-run, walk-off homer against Hall of Fame relief ace Dennis Eckersley to win Game 1 for the Dodgers, who rolled to a stunning World Series victory in five games over the favored Oakland A's.

1989: What made the first San Francisco Bay Series so memorable was the powerful earthquake that struck less than an hour before the start of Game 3 at Candlestick Park. The Series was postponed for ten days while a massive cleanup ensued on both sides of the Bay. When it resumed, the Oakland A's made quick work of the Giants, completing a four-game sweep.

1993: For only the second time in history, the World Series ended on a walk-off home run. It came off the bat of Toronto slugger Joe Carter and provided the Blue Jays with an 8–6 victory over the Phillies in the sixth and deciding game, and their second consecutive championship.

2000: Derek Jeter homered twice as the Yankees dismissed the Mets in five games in the first New York "Subway Series" since 1956. Luis Sojo's 2-run single in the ninth inning of Game 5 snapped a 2–2 tie and provided the Yankees with their fourth championship in 5 years and twenty-sixth overall.

2001: The September 11 attacks interrupted the final month of the season, pushing the World Series between the Yankees and the Arizona Diamondbacks into November for the first time. Game 3, the first Fall Classic game in New York since the horrific attacks, was of such symbolic importance that President George W. Bush threw out the ceremonial first pitch from the Yankee Stadium mound. Down 2–0, the Yankees won Games 3, 4, and 5 with the help of two-out, 2-run ninth-inning homers on consecutive nights by Tino Martinez and Scott Brosius. Behind the stalwart pitching of Randy Johnson and Curt Schilling, the Diamondbacks clinched the championship in only their fourth year of existence by winning the final two games in Arizona, including a ninth-inning Game 7 comeback against the great closer Mariano Rivera, capped by a Luis Gonzalez bloop single.

2002: In his first successful postseason, Barry Bonds appeared on the verge of delivering the Giants' first championship since they moved to San Francisco when the team took a 5–0 lead over Anaheim into the seventh inning of Game 6. But the Angels rallied for 3 runs in both the seventh and eighth innings to tie the Series at three wins apiece, and then coasted to a 4–1 victory in Game 7.

2004: On the brink of being swept by the Yankees in the ALCS, the Boston Red Sox rallied in the ninth inning of Game 4, and became the first team in baseball history to win a best-of-seven series after losing the first three games. They carried the momentum into and through the World Series, never trailing for an inning while sweeping the St. Louis Cardinals behind the hitting of Manny Ramirez (.412). The first championship for the Sox since 1918 was said to finally lift the so-called Curse of the Bambino.

Seven Wins

Cardinals pitcher Bob Gibson won seven World Series games, even though his team made only three trips to the Series. In one game he struck out seventeen batters.

words to know

bloop single

A weakly hit fly ball that drops in for a single between an infielder and an outfielder. It's also referred to as a bloop hit or a blooper.

fun fact

Marathon Match-Ups

Games 3 and 4 of the 2004 ALCS were two of the longest playoff games in history. The Yankees and the Red Sox played almost 11 hours of baseball in two days! But neither game holds the record for longest playoff game. In 2014, the Giants beat the Nationals after an exhilarating eighteen-inning game that ran for 6 hours and 23 minutes.

2010: Thirteen years after driving in the World Series–winning run for the Marlins in 1997, shortstop Édgar Rentería batted .412 and was honored as the MVP of the Giants' first championship in San Francisco. The Giants' outstanding pitching staff, led by Cy Young Award winner Tim Lincecum and relief ace Brian Wilson, limited the hard-hitting Rangers to 1 run and six hits over the final two games of the five-game Series.

2011: Although the Cardinals didn't qualify for the playoffs until the final day of the season, they earned their eleventh World Series title, the most by a National League club. Facing elimination in Game 6, they tied the Texas Rangers on David Freese's triple with two outs in the ninth inning. Down to the final strike once more in the tenth inning, they tied the score on Lance Berkman's single. Freese then homered in the eleventh to knot the Series at three wins apiece, and the Cardinals won Game 7, 6–2.

2012: After rallying from a 2–0 deficit in the NLDS and a 3–1 deficit in the NLCS, the Giants led from the start in the World Series. Third baseman Pablo Sandoval hit 3 homers in Game 1, including 2 off Detroit ace Justin Verlander, and the Giants swept the Tigers. Madison Bumgarner and Ryan Vogelsong started consecutive shutouts in Games 2 and 3.

2013: One year after finishing last in their division, the Boston Red Sox completed a remarkable turnaround with a World Series victory over the St. Louis Cardinals in six games. MVP David Ortiz dominated the offense with eleven hits and eight walks in twenty-five plate appearances for a stunning .760 on-base percentage, and starting pitcher Jon Lester allowed only 1 run in his two victories. It marked the team's third World Championship in 10 years but the first clinched in historic Fenway Park since 1918, when Babe Ruth was the pitching star.

2014: The Giants won their third title in 5 years over the Royals in seven games. The MVP was Giants pitcher Madison Bumgarner, whose performance was one of the best in World Series history. He won Games 1 and 5, including a complete-game shutout in Game 5. Two days later, in Game 7, Bumgarner threw five clean innings in relief, picking up the save in a tight 3–2 victory.

2015: Despite the heartbreaking Game 7 loss from the year before, the Kansas City Royals came back to play in the World Series in 2015. It was their first World Series win since 1985. The Mets took the lead in each of the five games; in four of them, though, the Royals came back to win, including Games 1 and 5 in extra innings. Royals catcher Salvador Perez was the first catcher to earn World Series MVP honors since 1992, when the Toronto Blue Jays' Pat Borders won the award.

fun fact

The Closer

Yankee relief pitcher John Wetteland became the first pitcher ever to save all four wins for his team in the 1996 World Series against Atlanta.

Name Change

In 1919, the Chicago White Sox were accused of being paid to lose the World Series! The scandal earned the team a nickname. Fill in all the letters that are **not** W-H-I-T-E to find out what it was.

BWLHAICTKESOX

Last Team Sitting

Every franchise in the National League has been represented at least once in the World Series. Fourteen of the fifteen clubs in the American League also have participated. The lone holdout as of 2022 is the Seattle Mariners, who began play in the 1977 season.

2016: For the first time in 108 years, the Cubs won the World Series. Despite being down 3–1 after four games, the Cubs came back and took the championship in one of the greatest Game 7s of all time, which included a rally in the bottom of the eighth, a short rain delay before extra innings, and a game-winning hit in the top of the tenth inning by World Series MVP Ben Zobrist.

2017: The Houston Astros, founded in 1962, won their first ever World Series four games to three. World Series MVP George Springer led the way with 5 home runs—tied for the most in any World Series by one player—including a home run in each of the last four games. In each of the first six games, the teams were within 2 runs of each other going into the ninth inning, making this one of the most exciting World Series ever.

2018: With dominant pitching from Chris Sale and David Price, and the AL MVP Mookie Betts leading the offense, the Boston Red Sox won the World Series four games to one over the Los Angeles Dodgers. Despite the Dodgers only winning one game, each game was closely fought, with Game 3 lasting a World Series record eighteen innings before Max Muncy hit a walk-off home run to win the game for the Dodgers. Alex Cora, in his first year managing the Red Sox, became the first Puerto Rican manager to win the World Series.

2019: For the first time in World Series history, the visiting team won every game. The victory by the Washington Nationals over the Houston Astros also marked the first championship for the team, which was founded as the Montreal Expos in 1969. It was also the first World Series win by a team representing the nation's capital since 1924 when the star was pitcher Walter Johnson. Fittingly, another tall right-handed pitcher, Stephen Strasburg, won two games and the MVP award.

2020: Because of the COVID-19 pandemic, the competition between the Los Angeles Dodgers and the Tampa Bay Rays was scheduled for a neutral site in Texas which

Secret Signals

Use the decoder to figure out what message the catcher signaled to the pitcher when the crab came up to bat.

A G N S C H

O T E I P U

F L R Y

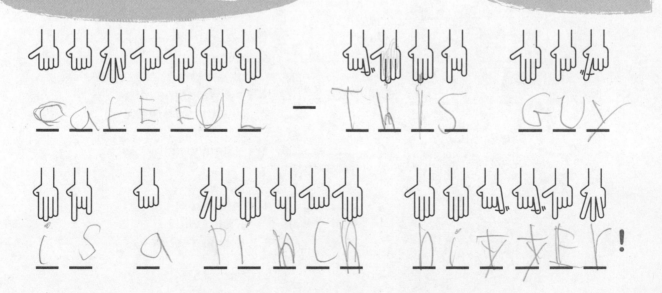

CAREFUL — THIS GUY

IS A PINCH HITTER!

allowed for a reduced number of spectators. Corey Seager, who batted .400 and played a flawless shortstop, led the Dodgers, making their third championship appearance in four seasons, to their first title in 32 years before an average crowd of 11,500 fans at Globe Life Field in Arlington.

2021: Jorge Soler, one of four players added in midseason who transformed the Braves' entire outfield, hit 3 home runs as Atlanta upset the Houston Astros in six games. Despite losing their best starting pitcher—Charlie Morton—to a broken leg in the first game, the Braves won their first world championship since 1995, and only their second since moving to the South 55 years earlier.

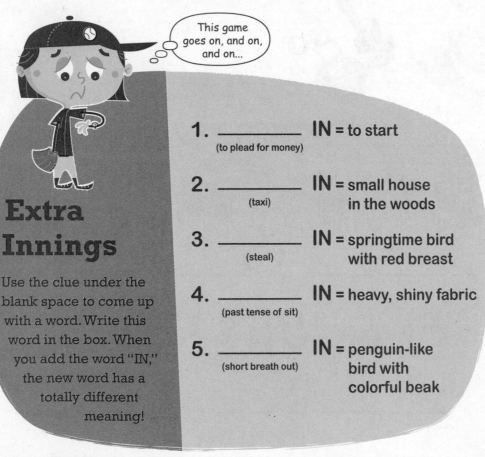

This game goes on, and on, and on...

Extra Innings

Use the clue under the blank space to come up with a word. Write this word in the box. When you add the word "IN," the new word has a totally different meaning!

1. _____ **IN** = to start
   (to plead for money)

2. _____ **IN** = small house
   (taxi) in the woods

3. _____ **IN** = springtime bird
   (steal) with red breast

4. _____ **IN** = heavy, shiny fabric
   (past tense of sit)

5. _____ **IN** = penguin-like
   (short breath out) bird with
   colorful beak

More than in any other sport, statistics are a big part of baseball. Since the beginning of the sport, fans have wanted to know who had the most hits, who made the error, who got the win, and so on. Home run totals, batting averages, wins, strikeouts—they are all a central part of baseball's popularity. Sometimes when a player was on the verge of breaking a record, like when Cal Ripken Jr. played in his 2,131st game, or when Hank Aaron hit home run number 715, or when Derek Jeter got his 3,000th hit, the individual achievements of the players got more attention than the ballgame. That's part of what makes baseball so interesting. Your team may not be doing well, like the Reds in the mid-1980s, but you might want to watch them anyway to see an all-time great like Pete Rose break a long-standing record.

There's a stat for everything in baseball. You could probably find the answer to "Which pitcher threw the most wild pitches in night games at Wrigley Field in the 1940s?" Okay, so that's a trick question—there were no night games at Wrigley in the 1940s because they had no lights. But the point is that if you love statistics you could probably spend a year looking at baseball statistics and never see the same one twice.

Individual Stats

Players' individual statistics, or "stats," are followed closely, not only by fans but also by sportswriters, team management, and everyone associated with baseball. There are actually thousands of statistics that are recorded, from how long it took to play a game to how many times a hitter grounded out to the shortstop. Many baseball stats, such as batting average or runs batted in, have been kept and published since the late nineteenth and early twentieth centuries. Others, like saves and holds, have been devised in more recent years.

Computers have made it easy to quickly calculate somewhat more obscure statistics, such as slugging percentage or batting average with runners in scoring position. The following are the most common player statistics you will see in the sports pages. Statistics for each game are usually found in what was termed back in the 1800s as a "box score," or a summary of the game in a box. More than 100 years later, whether you find box scores in the newspaper or online, they are still the most popular way to see what happened in a ballgame.

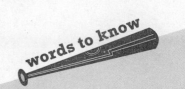

words to know

runs batted in (RBI)

A statistic that credits a batter for making a play that causes a run to be scored. The most common RBI is a hit that allows one or more players to score a run. Players also receive an RBI for a bases-loaded walk, or when being hit by a pitched ball results in a base runner advancing to score. A run that is scored as an error does not count as an RBI.

Box Score

On Monday, November 1, 2010, the San Francisco Giants and Texas Rangers played Game 5 of the World Series at Rangers Ballpark in Arlington, Texas. Going into the game, the Giants led the Series 3–1, so the Giants knew if they won the game, they would be World Champions. Super pitchers Cliff Lee and Tim Lincecum both pitched scoreless games through six innings. In the seventh, Giants shortstop Édgar Rentería hit a 3-run shot with two out, leading to a Giants championship.

Here's what you'd see in the box score for this game. Across the top is the inning-by-inning account of runs scored. You'll see that the Giants got 3 in the top of the seventh, but the Rangers could only get 1 in the bottom of the seventh.

You may wonder what this all means. Well, it's very simple once you learn about the format.

Box Scores

Team	1 2 3	4 5 6	7 8 9	R H E
San Francisco Giants	0 0 0	0 0 0	3 0 0	3 7 0
Texas Rangers	0 0 0	0 0 0	1 0 0	1 3 1

Giants

NAME	AB	R	H	RBI
Torres RF	4	0	1	0
Sanchez 2B	4	0	1	0
Posey C	4	0	2	0
Ross LF	4	1	1	0
Uribe 3B	4	1	1	0
Huff 1B	3	0	0	0
Burrell DH	4	0	0	0
Rentería SS	3	1	1	3
Rowand CF	3	0	0	0
Total	33	3	7	3

Rangers

NAME	AB	R	H	RBI
Andrus SS	4	0	0	0
Young 3B	4	0	1	0
Hamilton CF	4	0	0	0
Guerrero DH	4	0	0	0
Cruz RF	4	1	1	1
Kinsler 2B	2	0	0	0
Murphy LF	3	0	0	0
Molina C	3	0	0	0
Moreland 1B	2	0	1	0
Total	30	1	3	1

E – Moreland. GIDP – Rentería. LOB – San Francisco 4, Texas 4. HR – Rentería, Cruz. SAC – Huff.

PITCHERS

Giants

NAME	IP	H	R	ER	BB	SO
Lincecum (W, 4-1)	8	3	1	1	2	10
Wilson (S, 6)	1	0	0	0	0	2

Rangers

NAME	IP	H	R	ER	BB	SO
Lee (L, 3-2)	7	6	3	3	0	6
Feliz	2	1	0	0	0	2

Umpires: HP – Kellogg, 1B – Darling, 2B – Hirschbeck, 3B – Holbrook, LF – Miller, RF – Winters. Time of game – 2:32. Attendance: 52,045.

Across the top is the inning-by-inning account of runs scored.

R, H, and E are runs, hits, and errors for each team for the game.

The rest of the abbreviations are as follows:

Pos is the position that player played. If you see two people at the same position, that means the second player is a substitute.

The positions are:

1B	First base
2B	Second base
3B	Third base
SS	Shortstop
LF	Left fielder
CF	Center fielder
RF	Right fielder
C	Catcher
P	Pitcher
PH	Pinch hitter (someone who bats for another player)
PR	Pinch runner (someone who runs for someone else)
DH	The American League and some minor leagues use designated hitters, who bat for the pitchers. Since this game was played at an American League team's field, the DH was used.

The rest of the stats tell you what each player did in the game.

AB	At bats, or how many times the batter officially had a turn at bat (walks, sacrifices, and being hit by a pitch don't count as official at bats)
R	Runs scored
H	Hits

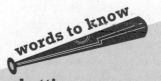

fun fact

The Ultimate Inning

In one game in 1999, Fernando Tatis of the St. Louis Cardinals hit a grand slam home run. His team kept on hitting and scoring runs in the inning, so he got to bat again in the same inning with the bases loaded. Believe it or not, he hit another grand slam, becoming the first player ever to hit 2 grand slam home runs and drive in 8 runs in one inning. Wow!

words to know

batting average

A player's hits divided by number of times at bat. A player's batting average is a good measure of his ability to hit. The best hitters have a .300 average or better, while a player hitting .200 might be sent back to the minor leagues.

fun fact

I'll Play Anywhere

Only two players in baseball history have played all ten positions. That's right, ten...Bert Campaneris of the A's and César Tovar of the Twins not only played all nine defensive positions, including one pitching appearance each, but they were also designated hitters.

words to know

sacrifice bunt

When a batter bunts to allow a runner to advance to another base. The hitter is almost always put out, but a sacrifice does not count statistically as a time at bat.

RBI	Runs batted in (a hit or another play that brings in runs)
BB	Base on balls (or walks)
SO	Strikeouts, also sometimes listed as "K"
AVG	Batting average

There will also be some information listed underneath the line that says "totals," telling you who hit doubles (2B), triples (3B), and home runs (HR), and how many of each the player has for the season or the playoffs. You'll also see if a player had a sacrifice (SAC) or a sacrifice fly (SF), or if he grounded into a double play (GIDP). Players don't like to see it, but there is also a listing of errors (E). Stolen bases (SB), caught stealing (CS), and runners the team left on base (LOB) are listed next. Many box scores may give you more detailed information, but these are the basics.

Pitching statistics are included toward the bottom. You'll often find next to pitchers' names the "decision," meaning the win (W) or loss (L), or the save (S) for a reliever. In the game previously described, Lincecum was the winning pitcher and Wilson earned the save. Lee was the losing pitcher. His win-loss record is listed as 3-2, or three wins and two losses for the playoffs.

Other numbers you may see next to the name are:

BS	Blown saves, which tell you how many times the pitcher has failed to save a game.
H	Hold, an unofficial statistic, will show up for relief pitchers. It means they held the lead until the closer came in and finished the game.

Then you'll see what is called the "pitcher's line" for the game, which includes:

IP   Innings pitched. Sometimes you'll see a decimal like 7.1, meaning the pitcher lasted seven innings and got one out in the eighth. 7.2 would mean he got two outs in the eighth.

H   Hits allowed

R   Runs allowed

ER   Earned runs allowed. Not all runs count as "earned runs." If an error on a play put a future scorer on base or helped a runner to score, that run does not count toward a pitcher's ERA. In the game mentioned earlier, the errors didn't allow any runs to score, so all runs were earned.

BB   Base on balls, or walks allowed

SO   Strikeouts (sometimes listed as "K")

ERA   The up-to-date earned run average of the pitcher, or how many earned runs he allows per nine innings. Pitchers try to keep their ERAs under 4.00. Starting pitchers pitch more innings, so it's harder for them to keep those ERAs down. An ERA under 3.50 is quite good, especially for a starting pitcher, and under 3.00 is excellent.

Now check out the newspaper or your favorite online sports site to find more box scores. Even if you didn't watch or listen to the game, you can figure out what happened or what your favorite player did. Reading box scores is the best way to keep up with what's happening in major league baseball.

words to know

ERA

A pitcher's "earned run average," or how many runs a pitcher is likely to give up in a full nine-inning game. To calculate ERA, multiply the number of earned runs allowed by nine; then divide by the number of innings pitched.

words to know

assist

When a player makes a throw of any kind to get an out, whether it's an infielder throwing out a batter at first base or an outfielder throwing out a runner at home plate.

Player Statistics

If you look up a player on the Internet or in a baseball book (including this one), you'll find ballplayers' statistics for each season and for their careers.

The most commonly found stats for hitters include everything in the box score and:

G	Games played
AVG	Batting average
SB	Stolen bases

You might also see SLG, or slugging percentage, which takes 1 point for each single, 2 for each double, 3 for each triple, and 4 for each home run, adds them up and divides by the number of at bats. Unlike batting averages, which rarely top .350, slugging percentages for the best power hitters can reach .600 or higher.

Common pitching stats include everything in the box score and:

G	Games pitched in
GS	Games started
CG	Complete games
SHO	Shutouts (held the opposing team to no runs)

The same statistics listed for a player can also be found for a team. The stats listed here are the basics, but you can find more in books that go into greater detail.

The Standings

To follow your favorite team, you can look in the newspaper at the sports pages or on a website like Baseball-Reference.com

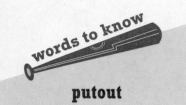

words to know

putout

Whenever a fielder performs an action that results in an out. Putouts can happen when a fielder catches a batted ball, steps on a base before a runner touches, or tags a batter who is not on a base. The catcher is credited with an out when catching the ball during a third strike.

fun fact

Shutouts

A pitcher earns a shutout by holding the opposing team without a run for the whole game. The pitcher who threw the most shutouts in baseball history was Walter Johnson, "the Big Train," who blanked the other team 110 times in his career.

to get plenty of information, including the standings—this means a list of the teams in first place through last place.

The major leagues today are each broken into three divisions:

American League

East	Central	West
Baltimore Orioles	Chicago White Sox	Houston Astros
Boston Red Sox	Cleveland Guardians	Los Angeles Angels
New York Yankees	Detroit Tigers	Oakland Athletics
Tampa Bay Rays	Kansas City Royals	Seattle Mariners
Toronto Blue Jays	Minnesota Twins	Texas Rangers

National League

East	Central	West
Atlanta Braves	Chicago Cubs	Arizona Diamondbacks
Miami Marlins	Cincinnati Reds	Colorado Rockies
New York Mets	Milwaukee Brewers	Los Angeles Dodgers
Philadelphia Phillies	Pittsburgh Pirates	San Diego Padres
Washington Nationals	St. Louis Cardinals	San Francisco Giants

Other Columns You May See in the Standings Chart

- **Division:** the team's record against teams in their own division
- **Home/Road:** the team's record when playing at their home park, and the team's record when playing away from home
- **Interleague:** the team's record in games against the other league

- **Streak:** how many games the team has won or lost in a row
- **Last 10:** the team's record in their last ten games

When you look at the standings in the papers, you'll see how many wins and losses the team has and their winning percentage, meaning what percentage of all the games they've played that they've won.

Fielding Percentage

One measure of a fielder's strength is the fielding percentage. To calculate this stat, add the player's putouts and assists. Then, divide by the total of the player's putouts, assists, and errors. A good fielder will have a fielding percentage of .980 or .990. Outfielders are expected to have higher fielding percentages than infielders.

Games Behind

When you look at the standings, you will also see the abbreviation "GB" (games behind), which is a way of judging how close your team is to first place in their division. Games behind means how many times your team would have to beat the first-place team in order to catch up with them. You might see:

Team	W-L	GB
New York Yankees	60-40	——
Boston Red Sox	58-42	2
Baltimore Orioles	54-48	7
Toronto Blue Jays	49-50	?
Tampa Bay Rays	40-60	?

How do you figure this out?

You subtract how many games the teams are apart in wins and then do the same for losses. In the first example, you can figure out the difference between the Yankees and Red Sox.

In wins you have 60 – 58 = 2.
In losses you have 42 – 40 = 2.
Then add the two numbers you came up with together: 2 + 2 = 4.

Then divide by 2: 4 ÷ 2 = 2.
The Red Sox are therefore 2 games behind the Yankees.

That one was easy because they were two games apart in wins and in losses. Sometimes teams will have played different numbers of games at a certain time in the season because of their schedules and because sometimes games are rained out.

To see how many games the Orioles are behind the Yankees, you would use the same formula.

Wins, 60 − 54 = 6.
Losses, 48 − 40 = 8.
Then add them together: 6 + 8 = 14.
Then divide by 2: 14 ÷ 2 = 7.
The Orioles are 7 games behind the Yankees.

Now, without looking below, try to figure out how far the Blue Jays are behind the Yankees.

Wins, 60 − 49 = 11.
Losses, 50 − 40 = 10.
11 + 10 = 21.
21 ÷ 2 = 10.5.

Now you try Tampa Bay! (In case you're wondering, Tampa Bay is 20 games out.)

words to know

sacrifice fly
When a batter hits a fly ball deep enough to allow a runner on third to tag up and score. A sacrifice fly does not count as a time at bat.

Lucky Numbers

Baseball is a game full of numbers. There are the RBI and ERA numbers, the numbers on the scoreboard, and of course the lucky number on the shirt of your favorite player!

In this tricky little puzzle, you must figure out what lucky combination of numbers to use so that each column (up and down) or row (across) adds up to the right totals shown in the white numbers. The white arrows show you in which direction you will be adding. Lucky you—four numbers are in place to get you started!

Here are the rules:

- **You are only adding the numbers in any set of white boxes that are touching each other.**

- **Use only the numbers 1 through 9. Each number can only be used *once* in each set.**

- **Remember that each answer has to be correct both across *and* down!**

All-Time Record Holders

These records are correct as of the end of the 2021 season.

Hitting

All-Time Batting Average Leaders

1. Ty Cobb .366
2. Rogers Hornsby .358
3. Shoeless Joe Jackson .356
4. Lefty O'Doul .349
5. Ed Delahanty .346
6. Tris Speaker .345
7. Ted Williams .344
8. Billy Hamilton .344
9. Dan Brouthers .342
10. Babe Ruth .342

A player must have more than 3,000 plate appearances to qualify for this list.

All-Time RBI Leaders

1. Hank Aaron 2,297
2. Babe Ruth 2,214
3. Albert Pujols 2,150
4. Alex Rodriguez 2,086
5. Cap Anson 2,075
6. Barry Bonds 1,996
7. Lou Gehrig 1,995
8. Stan Musial 1,951
9. Ty Cobb 1,944
10. Jimmie Foxx 1,922

All-Time Home Run Leaders

1. Barry Bonds 762
2. Hank Aaron 755
3. Babe Ruth 714
4. Alex Rodriguez 696
5. Albert Pujols 679
6. Willie Mays 660
7. Ken Griffey Jr. 630
8. Jim Thome 612
9. Sammy Sosa 609
10. Frank Robinson 586

Best Live-Ball ERA?

Most of the ERA leaders are from the "Dead-Ball Era," when the ball was softer and harder to hit with power. This era lasted until about 1920. So who of the more recent pitchers ranks best in ERA? Mariano Rivera, who comes in thirteenth of all time.

Position Players Wins Above Replacement (WAR)

1. Barry Bonds 162.8
2. Babe Ruth 162.1
3. Willie Mays 156.4
4. Ty Cobb 151.0
5. Hank Aaron 143.0
6. Tris Speaker 134.1
7. Honus Wagner 130.8
8. Stan Musial 128.2
9. Rogers Hornsby 127.0
10. Eddie Collins 124.0

Most Hits: Pete Rose at 4,256, followed by Ty Cobb at 4,189. They are the only two players with more than 4,000 hits!

Most Grand Slam Home Runs: Alex Rodriguez 25

Most Stolen Bases: Rickey Henderson 1,406

Most At Bats: Pete Rose 14,053

Most Seasons Played: Nolan Ryan 27

Pitching

All-Time Wins Leaders

1. Cy Young 511
2. Walter Johnson 417
3. Grover Alexander 373
4. Christy Mathewson 373
5. Warren Spahn 363
6. Kid Nichols 361
7. Pud Galvin 360
8. Greg Maddux 355
9. Roger Clemens 354
10. Tim Keefe 342

All-Time Strikeout Leaders

1. Nolan Ryan 5,714
2. Randy Johnson 4,875
3. Roger Clemens 4,672
4. Steve Carlton 4,136
5. Bert Blyleven 3,701
6. Tom Seaver 3,640
7. Don Sutton 3,574
8. Gaylord Perry 3,534
9. Walter Johnson 3,509
10. Greg Maddux 3,371

fun fact

Consecutive Scoreless Innings

Dodgers pitcher Orel Hershiser threw fifty-nine straight innings without giving up a run in September of 1988, breaking Dodger Don Drysdale's previous record.

Walks plus Hits per Inning Pitched (minimum 1,000 innings since 1900)

1. Addie Joss 0.967
2. Ed Walsh 0.999
3. Mariano Rivera 1.000
4. Clayton Kershaw 1.004
5. Jacob deGrom 1.011
6. Chris Sale 1.042
7. Pedro Martinez 1.054
8. Christy Mathewson 1.058
9. Trevor Hoffman 1.058
10. Walter Johnson 1.061

Pitchers Wins Above Replacement (WAR)

1. Cy Young 165.6
2. Walter Johnson 151.6
3. Roger Clemens 138.7
4. Kid Nichols 116.5
5. Grover Alexander 115.9
6. Lefty Grove 113.3
7. Tom Seaver 106.0
8. Greg Maddux 104.8
9. Randy Johnson 103.5
10. Christy Mathewson 97.6

Lowest All-Time ERA: (2,000 or more innings) Ed Walsh 1.82

Most All-Time Saves: Mariano Rivera at 652 (saves became an official statistic in 1969)

Most No-Hitters: Nolan Ryan 7

Manager Wins

The manager with the most all-time wins is Connie Mack, who won 3,731 games over 53 years between 1894 and 1950. His record has a lot to do with the many years he was a manager—he actually lost more games than he won! On the other hand, Joe McCarthy managed teams to 2,125 wins, but he only lost 1,333 games for a winning percentage of .615—the best of all time.

WHIP

An abbreviation that stands for "Walks plus Hits per Inning Pitched," and means almost the same thing as base runners per inning. Only the very best pitchers' WHIPs are below 1.000. A good WHIP is 1.100 or 1.150.

How come Drew never finishes a baseball game?

To find out, cross out all the words that have three letters or the letter U!

AND	EVERY	CAT
TIME	GOT	HE
BAT	GETS	FAR
TO	FUR	THIRD
BUT	BASE	HIT
HE	HAT	GOES
HUT	HOME	BAG

One-Season Records

Hitting (after 1900)

Most Doubles: Earl Webb 67, Boston Red Sox 1931

Most Triples: Chief Wilson 36, Pittsburgh Pirates 1912

Most Home Runs: Barry Bonds 73, San Francisco Giants 2001

Most Runs Batted In: Hack Wilson 191, Chicago Cubs 1930

Most Hits: Ichiro Suzuki 262, Seattle Mariners 2004

Highest Batting Average (500+ Plate Appearances): Rogers Hornsby .424, St. Louis Cardinals 1924

Most Stolen Bases: Ricky Henderson 130, Oakland Athletics 1980

Pitching (after 1900)

Most Wins: Jack Chesbro 41, New York Highlanders 1904

Most Strikeouts: Nolan Ryan 383, California Angels 1973

Lowest Earned Run Average: Dutch Leonard 0.96, Boston Red Sox 1914

Most Shutouts: Grover Alexander 16, Philadelphia Phillies 1916

Most Saves: Francisco Rodriguez 62, Los Angeles Angels 2008

Lowest WHIP: Pedro Martinez 0.737, Boston Red Sox 2000

Highest WAR: Walter Johnson 16.5, Washington Senators 1913

Chapter 8
Beyond the Major Leagues

Baseball fans love to go to major league games as well as watch, read, and tell stories about their favorite teams. But you can enjoy baseball even if you're not watching the Yankees or the Astros. You can watch minor-league, high school, or college baseball—in fact, these teams are sometimes even more fun to follow, because you can get closer to the action and to the players. Fast-pitch softball is another exciting game to watch, and you can follow high school or college teams, as well as at the professional level.

Getting to the Majors

Everyone knows that major league baseball players are the best in the world. But *how* do the teams know they're getting the best players? It's not like just anyone can stop by Busch Stadium and ask for a tryout! Before a player makes it to the major leagues, he's played baseball for 10–15 years. He's played in youth leagues, in high school, probably in a summer league, maybe in college, and in the minor leagues. Teams watch players at each of these levels to find out who they think they want on their major league team.

Professional vs. Amateur

A professional baseball player is paid to play; an amateur baseball player volunteers to play for a team for fun, or to improve his skills. Major leaguers are professionals, but so are players in the minor leagues. College and high school players are amateurs.

High School Baseball

Though their games don't usually draw thousands of fans like the football games do, most every high school in the country fields a baseball team. The season usually starts in March, earlier in warm-weather areas like Florida, and finishes in late May. High school teams play about twenty games per season.

Becoming a Professional Baseball Player: The Draft

Major league teams are always scouting, sending out expert watchers to find out who the best young players are. The thirty teams get competitive with each other to convince the best teenagers to play for them.

A player who was born in the United States or Canada cannot choose which team to play for. First, he has to enter a draft. In June, teams take turns picking players, just like you might pick teams on the playground. A high school graduate who is picked, say, by the Mariners has three choices:

- He can sign a contract with the Mariners. In this case, he must stay with the Mariners until he's played 6 years in the major leagues (or until he's traded to a different team).
- He can refuse to sign a contract with the Mariners and instead wait a year to re-enter the draft to be chosen by a different team.
- He can refuse to sign with the Mariners and instead go to college. In this case, he has to play in college for 3 years before re-entering the draft.

A player who was not born in the United States or Canada, or a player who entered the draft but wasn't drafted by anyone, can choose to sign a contract with any team. Once he signs a contract, he belongs to that team until he's played 6 years in the majors.

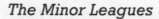

Does Anyone Skip the Minor Leagues?

Very rarely, a player is signed who is ready to play in the major leagues right away. Cincinnati pitcher Mike Leake went straight from college to the Reds in 2010. Before that, in 2000, Xavier Nady went straight from college to the Padres. Everyone else in those 10 years played at least some minor league baseball.

The Minor Leagues

A player who signs an initial contract with a major-league team probably isn't ready to play for that team yet. Pretty much everyone starts his career in the minor leagues.

Minor league teams play in smaller towns with smaller stadiums than major league teams. They travel short distances to play their away games, but they travel by bus, not the fancy private jets that major league teams get.

Each major league team supports a bunch of minor-league teams at different levels. Drafted players usually start at the lowest levels, called "Rookie League" and "Class A." The best players at each level get to move up a level after a year or so. The top minor league level is called "AAA," or "triple-A." The best players on a team's AAA team can be called up to the majors.

Dugout

One letter has been dug out of each of the following common baseball words. Fill in the missing letters. Then, transfer those letters to the corresponding boxes in the grid to form the answer to this riddle:

What's another nickname for a baseball bat?

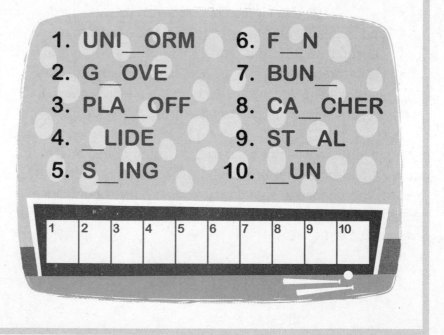

1. UNI__ORM
2. G__OVE
3. PLA__OFF
4. __LIDE
5. S__ING

6. F__N
7. BUN__
8. CA__CHER
9. ST__AL
10. __UN

1	2	3	4	5	6	7	8	9	10

College Baseball

Most sports fans have watched college football and college basketball. College baseball can be just as exciting, especially in June during the College World Series.

College baseball teams are made up of students, though many of these students have scholarships that pay for them to go to school. They play about sixty games each year, starting around February and finishing in May.

After the end of the regular season, sixty-four teams are chosen for the NCAA tournament. They are divided into groups of four teams, which each play a double-elimination tournament over a weekend in early June. These first round games are called the "regionals."

The winners of the regionals are paired the next weekend for the "superregionals." Whichever team is the first to win two games in the superregionals gets to go to the College World Series (CWS).

The College World Series is held in Omaha, Nebraska, every year. The eight teams who won their superregionals play two double-elimination tournaments. The winners of each of these mini-tournaments play each other in a best-of-three series for the National Championship.

All of the CWS games are played at the same stadium in Omaha. The teams and their fans take over the city for two weeks in June, using up all of the space in the local hotels. One special part of the CWS is the friendliness that develops among fans of all the teams. Since there are games every day in the same place, and since it's summertime when schools are out, the fans can get to know each other as part of a baseball vacation.

The Show

Some college players, and all minor leaguers, are trying to make baseball their career. They say their goal is to "make it to the Show," which is slang for the major leagues.

NCAA

Baseball, like other sports, is an important part of college life. NCAA stands for the National Collegiate Athletic Association. The NCAA was founded in 1906 primarily to govern football, but now this organization runs all sports played by its member schools.

How Does a Double-Elimination Tournament Work?

"Double-elimination" means that a team plays until they lose twice. Four teams start the tournament by playing a game. The next day, the teams that won play against each other, and the teams that lost play each other. After the second day, one team will have lost twice—they're out. Two teams will have lost only once; they play each other, and the loser is out. The two remaining teams play each other until one of those teams has two losses. The team that's left is the winner.

Women in Baseball

Women's place in professional baseball has rarely been on the field. But there was a time when their participation was not only encouraged but considered essential. Midway through World War II, the All-American Girls Professional Baseball League (AAGPBL) began play.

The league was sponsored by Philip K. Wrigley, the owner of the Chicago Cubs, who grew concerned that interest in major league baseball was waning because so many of its stars were serving in the armed forces. Consisting of teams from smaller cities throughout the Midwest, the AAGPBL employed more than six hundred female athletes during its existence from 1943 through 1954.

A League of Their Own, a 1992 movie based loosely on the experiences of players during that time, reminded later generations of its historic importance. Although there was no real Dottie Hinson, the main character of the movie, there was a Dorothy ("Dottie" or "Kammie") Kamenshek, who was the all-star first base player of the Rockford Peaches and was listed among the top one hundred female athletes of the twentieth century by *Sports Illustrated*.

There wasn't another attempt at professional baseball for women until 1994 when the Colorado Silver Bullets team was founded by former Atlanta Braves executive Bob Hope with the financial backing of the Coors Brewing Company. Managed by Hall of Fame pitcher Phil Niekro, the team played 195 games against amateur and semi-pro men's teams over 4 years before the sponsor withdrew its support.

Meanwhile, women's baseball was sanctioned in the US by the Amateur Athletic Union in 2003 and has flourished in many other countries. A team representing the US has competed in the first eight Women's Baseball World Cup tournaments, winning the first two; Japan dominated the next six championships. The tournament now includes twelve nations.

The Magic Number

Near the end of the baseball season teams start to figure out the "magic number." This is how many games the leading team must win, and how many games any other team must lose, for the leader to win the pennant (championship in their league).

There's some tricky math here. Pretend you have two teams—Team A and Team X. Team A is the leading team in the league, having won the most games so far. Team X is any other team in the league.

Follow the steps below using the scores from our sample teams. You can use the same steps with your favorite teams!

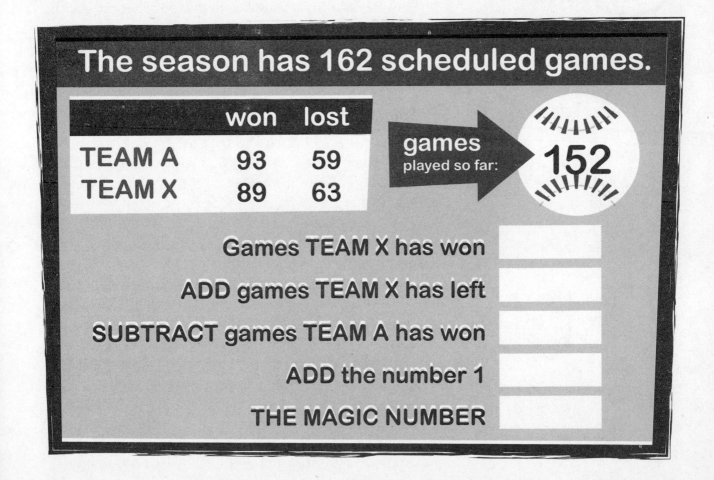

The season has 162 scheduled games.

	won	lost
TEAM A	93	59
TEAM X	89	63

games played so far: 152

Games TEAM X has won

ADD games TEAM X has left

SUBTRACT games TEAM A has won

ADD the number 1

THE MAGIC NUMBER

Women in MLB

Although women have yet to earn a place on a major-league roster, they have made inroads in other areas. Two former softball stars—Rachel Balkovec and Rachel Folden—were employed as batting coaches for minor league clubs of the Yankees and Cubs, respectively, in 2021. Alyssa Nakken is an assistant coach for the Giants and, most significantly, Kim Ng began her first season as general manager of the Marlins in 2021.

While there are more than two hundred women among the more than four thousand persons working in major league baseball operations, Ng ascended to the top of her profession only after 30 years in the business. Two other women, Jean Afterman and Raquel Ferreira, serve as assistant general manager of MLB teams, the Yankees and Red Sox, respectively.

Softball

While the term "softball" wasn't used widely until 1930, the sport dates back to 1887 when a member of Chicago's Farragut Boat Club tossed a rolled-up boxing glove at another member, who responded by hitting it with a broomstick. The club devised rules for the game which soon became popular throughout the city and the entire Midwest under the name of "indoor baseball."

Softball soon moved outdoors and became wildly successful among both men and women after a set of standardized rules were implemented in the 1930s. While men had the option of baseball, women who chose to play ball were steered to the newer sport and benefitted by the establishment of the Amateur Softball Association (ASA) in 1933.

Perhaps the most famous club of the post–World War II era was the Brakettes. Founded in 1947 and sponsored by the Raybestos brake company of Stratford, Connecticut, the Brakettes won twenty-eight of the next sixty ASA national championships, including eight in a row during the 1970s. Their brightest star was Joan Joyce, a pitcher whose amateur record of 507-33 included 123 no-hitters, thirty-three perfect games, and a .327 batting average. Most famously, she struck out Ted Williams, among the greatest baseball hitters in history, in a charity event the year after he retired.

Joan Joyce's individual success convinced tennis star Billie Jean King and other organizers to form the International Women's Professional Softball Association in 1976. As the star player, manager, and part-owner of the Connecticut Falcons, Joyce led her team to the title in all four seasons before the league folded. Another generation of stars—Dot Richardson, Lisa Fernandez, and Jennie Finch, among them—set the standards for more recent professional leagues.

The Women's Pro Softball League lasted from 1997 until 2001. Starting in 2004, the National Pro Fastpitch League survived until 2021 when it shut down because of the COVID-19 pandemic. Yet, the sport continues to grow through the popularity of the college game and an NCAA postseason sixty-four-team tournament similar in format to the men's baseball championship.

Baseball Across the World

When a relief pitcher from Australia closed the 2021 All-Star Game, saving the victory for Japanese starter Shohei Ohtani, the Aussie was not surprised. "It's a world game now," Liam Hendriks said.

So it is. The popularity of baseball has spread halfway around the planet, as well as to a few stops in between. There are several reasons for that, starting with a tour by the great Babe Ruth and other major league all-stars to Japan in 1934 and the subsequent US involvement in that nation after World War II. Baseball also has gained a hold in

Taiwan, South Korea, and other Asian outposts, as well as Australia, virtually all the Caribbean countries, and some parts of South America.

Baseball was included at the Olympic Games for the first time in 1992. As evidence of the rising quality of play outside the US, an American team (denied the use of current major leaguers by Olympic rules) won the gold medal only once in the next five Olympics. The sport was omitted from the 2012 Games in London and the 2016 Games in Rio but readmitted in 2021 at Tokyo where Japan defeated the US.

Partially in reaction to the temporary Olympic snub, organized baseball created the World Baseball Classic, where the best major leaguers are given the opportunity to represent their native homelands in a tournament staged in the spring every 4 years.

If your love of baseball goes beyond a seat in the bleachers or on the living room couch, there are many ways to add more baseball to your life. Think about joining a fantasy league or creating one with your friends. Invest in trading cards just for the fun of it and maybe the one-in-a-million chance of finding a true collector's item. Learn how to score a game the way broadcasters, sportswriters, and statisticians do so you can go back and replay each at bat hours, weeks, or months later. For super fans like you, there's more to baseball than just, well, baseball!

Fantasy Baseball

Have you ever wanted to own a baseball team? If so, you should start saving your money now—it costs close to $1.9 billion to buy an average major league team. But you and your friends can run your own fantasy baseball teams this season without paying any money at all.

In fantasy baseball, you choose major league players to be on your team. The better your players perform, the better your team does. Since you're in charge of your team, you can make trades, bench players who aren't doing well, set starting lineups, put players on the disabled list—pretty much everything a real baseball owner does.

How Fantasy Baseball Works

Fantasy baseball teams get points based on how well a player does in real life. Each day, you have to go in and set your starting lineup. Make sure you're not starting anyone who isn't playing that day! Your team gets credit for the statistics of all the players in your starting lineup. If one of your players hits a home run in the game he's playing in real life, your team gets a home run. If one of your pitchers strikes out eight batters, your team adds eight strikeouts to its total.

One major difference between real baseball and fantasy baseball is that defense doesn't matter in fantasy. There aren't enough defensive statistics. You want hitters who are really good at the plate or pitchers who rack up a lot of strikeouts. Don't worry if they're not good at fielding ground balls or catching pop-ups.

Fantasy Team Rosters

Your team usually looks similar to a real major league lineup, with a few differences. Using the standard settings on *Yahoo! Fantasy* as an example, you have a catcher, first baseman, second baseman, third baseman, and shortstop, just like in real baseball. You have three outfielders, too, though they don't have to be a right fielder, a center fielder, and a left fielder. You could have three right fielders if you wanted, or a center fielder and two left fielders! You'll also see one or two slots for a utility player. This can be any offensive player you want, at any position. Think of it like the DH for fantasy.

For pitching, you usually have two spots for starting pitchers, two spots for relief pitchers, and four general pitcher spots. You can put either starting pitchers or relief pitchers in the general pitcher spots.

You also have about five bench spots. These are players who are on your team but don't count toward your final score. If one of your bench players does really well, it can be a bit of a bummer that they don't count. But consider playing him the next day in case he does well again!

Different Types of Leagues

All right, now you know the basics of fantasy baseball. You know what it is and how many players you have on your team. Now you need to know how to keep score. There are two basic types of fantasy baseball leagues with slightly different rules: head-to-head and rotisserie (also known as "roto").

In head-to-head fantasy leagues, you play a "game" against another team in your league each week. You have to do better than your opponent in each category. For example, if your pitchers record five saves this week and your opponent's pitchers only record four saves, then you win the "saves" category. If you win more categories than your opponent, then you win the week! Whichever team wins the most games by the end of the year is the champion.

In rotisserie leagues, you keep track of all your statistics for the whole season. Then you rank each person in each category and give them points for how well they did. Whoever gets the most points at the end of the season after adding up all the categories is the league champion.

Determining Who's on Your Team

All fantasy baseball owners want Mike Trout or Shohei Ohtani on their team. But a star player can only be on one team in each league. So how do you decide who gets which players? Well, there are three ways to get a player: through the draft, picking them up off the waiver wire, or trading for them.

The Draft

At the beginning of the season, before any real MLB games are played, fantasy team owners get together and draft their teams. There are two common types of drafts: the

fun fact

One Win or Ten?

In head-to-head leagues, there are two kinds of scoring. You can score each week as a win or a loss, so a team can be 1-0 or 0-1 after one week. The other way to count the scoring is by the number of categories each team wins. So if you win four of the ten categories, instead of being 0-1, you'd be 4-6. Each type of scoring is fun in its own way, so give both a try!

snake draft and the auction draft. The snake draft is simpler and is the best way to go if you're new to fantasy baseball. In a snake draft, teams take turns selecting players. On your turn, you can choose any player who hasn't already been chosen. But you have to be sure to fill every position on your team! It's called a snake draft because the order of who gets to pick "snakes" back and forth each round. If you have the first pick in one round, you'll have the last pick in the next.

In an auction, each team is given a budget of pretend money—say, $2,000—to buy the players they want. A player is nominated and then each team can bid for that player. Whoever bids the most money gets the player. But you only have that $2,000 for your whole team. If you spend too much on one player, you'll be stuck without money to fill out your roster. You could get two top players like Vladimir Guerrero Jr. and Jacob deGrom, which is difficult to do in a snake draft, but then the rest of your team would probably be pretty weak since you would have very little money left.

Waivers

The draft isn't the only way to get players. After all, if one of your players gets hurt or isn't doing well, you'll need to replace him. The easiest way to pick up players during the season is through "waivers." Players who aren't on anyone's team in the fantasy league are listed on the "waiver wire." If you want to add a player, you can choose someone from this list to be on your team. But you can only have a certain number of players on your roster, so if you want to add a player from the waiver wire, you have to drop someone from your team. Don't be too hasty about dropping a player who had one bad week. Maybe they're just in a slump and will come out of it soon. Only drop a player if you think they're not going to be as good as the player you're picking up for the rest of the season.

> **fun fact**
>
> ### Use a Cheat Sheet
>
> Rankings of the best players are called "cheat sheets." Don't start a draft without one! You can make cheat sheets yourself or you can use one from a magazine or website. Don't worry about the name—it's not really cheating to have one!

Trades

Another option for improving your team is to make trades. If your team has plenty of one statistic but needs to do better in another, you can swap players with another team to help even everything out, as long as the other team agrees. For example, your team might have a whole lot of stolen bases but not very many saves. So, you could offer to give another team a fast runner, like Trea Turner, in exchange for a closer like Josh Hader.

A good strategy for trading is to look for players who are having a bad stretch of play but are likely to turn it around soon. If a player you really like is going through a bit of a slump, talk to their owner and see who they want for him. Who knows? Maybe the owner is disappointed that the player did poorly last week and wants to get rid of him. Then, if they turn it around and break out of their slump, you have another good player on your team.

Fantasy Baseball Strategy

The fantasy team owners who do the best are the ones who pay careful attention to the players. Sure, you want to pick star players, the guys everyone knows about. But soon after your draft starts, there won't be any stars left. So how do you know which players to pick?

Before your draft, you should read about every team. Find out which new players are on the team. Know who is likely to start at each position for each team. Then make a list of who you think are the best ten or fifteen major league players at each position, and a list of the thirty or so players you absolutely want if you can get them.

As you go through the draft, figure out a strategy for who you should take in each round. If you already have two really good outfielders, maybe you can wait to take your third one until you fill up a few spots in your infield. Or if there's only one pitcher you really like left when it comes time to pick, grab him to make sure someone else doesn't take him. There are also a lot of rankings online that will tell you where players are being drafted by other people. If you know a player isn't usually being drafted until the tenth round in a snake draft, you don't have to take him in the third round. It's not likely that another team will grab him that early.

Weekly Strategy

Once you've played a few weeks, you'll start to get a feel for who your really good players are and who isn't as good. You'll want to keep your really good players in the lineup every day they're playing. Only take them out if their team has the day off. For the players who aren't as good, each day you'll have to decide if you want to put them in your starting lineup or bench them for one of your other players.

To help you decide who to play, take a look at what team they're playing against and who's pitching against them. If they're facing an average pitcher, an average hitter is more likely to get a few hits and maybe even a home run. But if they're facing Gerrit Cole, you might want to start your best hitters. Also look at how they've been doing lately. Even if they're not a star, a player can go on a hot streak and help you win your matchup. If they're facing a good pitcher but have been doing really, really well lately, maybe they can still contribute.

Baseball Cards

Baseball cards are the size of playing cards. They have a picture of a player on one side; the other side lists his career stats and a short description of his career highlights. Your card collection is a reflection of your favorite teams and your favorite players, but as you get older, your collection can help you remember past seasons.

Acquiring Baseball Cards

You can buy baseball cards in lots of different places, like department stores, drug stores, or online sites. Specialist card stores, dealers, and sellers on *eBay* might have rare or especially interesting cards.

Cards come in packs of several cards. Many companies make baseball cards, each with a different look. Topps, Panini America, and Upper Deck are among the most popular card-making companies. Most packs include a random assortment of current players—the fun is seeing which players you get when you open the pack. New cards come out every season, as they have since the early 1900s.

Most card buyers enjoy collecting the cards for the fun of it. The cards themselves have a glossy look and the photos are sometimes really cool action shots from a game. The statistics on the back of the cards give you all sorts of information about how the player has done in his career. Reading your cards can teach you a lot about your favorite players, so the next time you see them in a game, you have a better appreciation for who they are and how far they've come.

There are more serious collectors who buy and sell older or special cards for lots of money. But baseball card collecting is not about monetary value—it's about savoring the game of baseball. Many of the wealthy collectors who have turned a youthful hobby into an expensive pastime started in the same way as you, by breathlessly opening a small pack and hoping for the best.

Collectible Cards

Sometimes the most valuable cards are those that accidentally get printed with a few mistakes or differences. Can you find the nine differences between these two cards?

Collectible Words

See if you can collect nine words hiding in the word **COLLECTIBLE**.

Extra Fun: Try to have all nine words use only four letters.

commons

Baseball cards of average players, not superstars. These cards aren't usually valuable to professional collectors, but they still might have value to you if the player is one of your favorites.

Stick of Gum

Once upon a time, one of the things you would always find in a pack of baseball cards was a long, pink stick of chewing gum. This isn't very common anymore, but it was standard for many years.

Some Baseball Card History

Professional baseball began at the end of the 1860s, and the first baseball cards were printed by the late 1880s. These early cards were printed on the cardboard backs of cigarette packs. Top players of the day like Cap Anson and Buck Ewing were among the first players to appear on cards. By the early 1900s, a number of cigarette manufacturers were printing cards of the best players, such as Ty Cobb and Honus Wagner. There were far fewer copies of each card printed than there are of cards today.

By the 1930s chewing gum companies were also making baseball cards, and collecting these cards was becoming more popular. The Goudey Gum Company produced a 240-card set called "Big League Chewing Gum," placing numbered cards with a small slab of bubble gum in each pack. In 1933, fans who bought cards all season as they tried to collect a complete set realized that there was no number 106 card. So many collectors sent letters asking for the missing card that the company had to print more in 1934, and it sent them to the people who had written in. This was one of the first indications that card collecting was becoming popular. That 106 card celebrated all-star (and future Hall of Famer) Nap Lajoie, and it became one of the most valuable cards of the era.

Then, in 1952, Topps made its first baseball cards with statistics of the players on the back. Card collecting was very popular through the 1960s and 1970s, but it wasn't until the late 1980s that rich collectors began to pay high prices for old cards. Some people began to see baseball cards as an investment, like putting money in the stock market. Today, baseball card sets no longer contain gum, and card collecting isn't quite as popular as it was at the start of the 1990s, but many, many fans still savor their collections.

What Should You Do with Your Baseball Cards?

The easy answer to that question is—anything you want, especially anything that makes collecting cards fun. Here are some ideas of ways to enjoy your collection.

- **Read your cards.** You may think you know everything about your favorite player, but you might be surprised by some new information on that player's card. You might learn something about a player that makes you like him more—for example, he may have grown up in your hometown, or he may have gone to your favorite college.
- **Trade with your friends.** If you are buying lots of packs of cards, you will end up with several copies of the same player's card. Offer to give a duplicate to a friend if your friend will give you a card that you really want. Or, say you're trying to collect the whole starting lineup for your favorite team. You might be able to fill in the cards you don't have by trading.
- **Use cards as decorations.** Is the wall behind your desk or over your bed bare? Does your locker need something on the door? Use baseball cards to decorate. You could change the players you have on display every month or every year based on how the players do.
- **Get autographs.** If you know that you might have a chance to get a player's autograph—say, you have front-row tickets to a game, or you're going to hear a player speak—bring that player's card and ask him to sign it.

 *fun fact*

The Most Expensive Card Ever

Pirates shortstop Honus Wagner did not want his card associated with cigarettes, so he asked that the tobacco company stop printing his cards. Therefore, only a few cards of this legendary player exist. His 1909 card, known to collectors as T206, is so rare that at an online auction in 2016 one sold for $3.1 million. That record-high sale price has been surpassed three times in recent years, first by a 2009 Bowman Chrome prospects card of the Angels' Mike Trout ($3.9 million) in August 2020. Five months later, a 1952 Topps card of Yankees' superstar Mickey Mantle went for $5.2 million, only to be surpassed in August 2021 when a Honus Wagner card was sold in a private sale for a reported $6.6 million.

Name Game

This baseball card collector has gotten some pretty famous autographs. Unfortunately, the players signed their names too big! Can you tell who signed each card? Choose names from the list.

Barry Bonds

Willie Mays

Nolan Ryan

Pete Rose

Alex Rodriguez

Cy Young

Sandy Koufax

Ty Cobb

Jimmie Foxx

Tom Seaver

Greg Maddux

Lou Gehrig

Hank Aaron

Keeping Score

Keeping score is a fun way to keep track of what's happening on the field, and it will give you a lasting record of the game you watched. You can buy scorecards at the ballpark or make your own on a sheet of graph paper. To make life a little easier, you can use the scorecard in Chapter 7 of this book as a model. The most important thing is that you have a place to write the name of each player and boxes for all nine (or more) innings so that you can write down what they do with each at bat. Names run down the left side of the page and innings run across the top. Why not try scoring the next game you go to?

Scoring Symbols

Scoring is pretty easy once you know the symbols to put in the boxes. You are writing down what the batter does each time he bats. Most of the time you will be listing hits, walks, or outs. When the batter makes an out, he either hit the ball to a fielder, or he struck out. For scoring purposes, the fielders are numbered. This number has nothing to do with the numbers the players are wearing on their uniforms; instead, it describes the position played by each player:

Numbers for fielding
1. Pitcher
2. Catcher
3. First baseman
4. Second baseman
5. Third baseman
6. Shortstop
7. Left fielder
8. Center fielder
9. Right fielder

The First Scorecard

The first scorecard was created by the Knickerbocker ball club way back in 1845.

Scorebooks

A scorebook is a book full of scorecards. Some people keep score of their favorite team's games in the same book all year. Some families take a scorebook to all the games they attend, then ask players to autograph the pages. You can buy scorebooks at sporting goods stores.

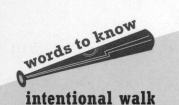

intentional walk

When a pitcher walks a batter on purpose. Sometimes this makes it easier to get a double play if there are other runners on second and/or third. Sometimes a batter is walked intentionally because the player is very good and the pitcher doesn't want to give up a home run. An intentional walk is scored as "IW" or "IBB" (intentional base on balls).

Let's say the ball is hit in the air to the center fielder and he makes the catch for an out. You would put "8" in the box on your scorecard to show that the center fielder made the out. If the ball went to right field, you'd put "9," and if it's a pop-up to the first baseman, you'd put "3."

If the ball is hit on the ground to the shortstop and he throws to first, you put down both numbers since they were both part of the play. Therefore, a groundout to shortstop would be "6-3." A groundout to the second baseman, who throws it to third base to get an advancing runner, would be "4-5." Remember, you want to include all of the players who help get an out on the play, so a double play that goes from the shortstop to the second baseman to the first baseman would be scored "DP 6-4-3."

Hits can be scored in a few ways. A single is either "1B" or a single line (–), a double is "2B" or a double line (=), a triple is "3B" or a triple line (≡), and a home run is "HR" or four lines (≣).

When runners get on base, you keep track of them using the diamond in the box on the scorecard. Just draw a line along the base path for each base they get to. For example, if a player reaches first base, you would draw the line going from home to first base. If he moves to second base when the next hitter gets a single, you would add a line going from first base to second base. If a player is tagged out or stranded on base at the end of the inning, you just leave the diamond incomplete.

Other Scoring Symbols

More things happen in baseball games than just hits and outs. Here is a more thorough list of the common scoring symbols. To use these, just write the symbol in the box of the player who was out or advanced a base.

BB   Base on balls, or you can write "W" for walk

K   Strikeout. If the batter struck out looking (meaning he just stood there while the umpire called a pitch over home plate for strike three), then you can write a backward "K."

HBP   Hit batter

SF   Sacrifice fly

S or SAC   Sacrifice bunt

E#   Error, followed by the number of the fielder who made the error. For example, an error by the second baseman would be written "E4."

DP   Double play (including the fielder numbers involved in the play)

TP   Triple play (including the fielder numbers involved in the play). Triple plays are extremely rare, so if you score one of these, save the scorecard.

SB   Stolen base

L   Line drive

F   Usually means that the ball was in foul territory when it was caught. A foul pop-up to the catcher would be scored "2F."

Other symbols you might use that don't describe what the batter did but often tell you that the runners moved up can be put in a corner of the box:

SB   Stolen base

CS   Caught stealing (include the fielder numbers involved in the play)

PB   Passed ball—this is when the catcher drops a ball he should have caught, allowing a runner to advance

WP   Wild pitch—this is when a pitch is so bad that the catcher didn't have a good chance to catch it, and a runner advances

words to know

commentators

The broadcasters or announcers who are at the ballpark describing what is going on in the game for television or radio broadcasts or online streaming. They keep detailed scorecards so they can tell the audience what has happened in the game.

fun fact

Dropped Third Strikes

When first base is open or when there are two outs, the catcher must hold on to the third strike. If the ball hits the ground before he catches it, he must get the out by tagging the batter or throwing to first base. Usually, the catcher does this without trouble. However, if the third strike was a wild pitch, or if the catcher makes a bad throw to first, the runner could be safe, but the pitcher still gets statistical credit for a strikeout. If this happens, on your scorecard you would write "K-E2" (if the catcher made a bad throw) or "K-WP" (if the pitcher made a wild pitch).

Glossary

assist

When a player makes a throw of any kind to get an out, whether it's an infielder throwing out a batter at first base or an outfielder throwing out a runner at home plate.

base hit

When a batter hits a ball into fair territory and gets to first, second, or third base.

batter's box

The area in front of home plate where a batter must stand while at bat.

batting average

A player's hits divided by number of times at bat. A player's batting average is a good measure of his ability to hit. The best hitters have a .300 average or better, while a player hitting .200 might be sent back to the minor leagues.

batting order

The order in which players on a team come up and take their turn as the hitter. The manager or coach of the team decides the batting order before the game and lists the players, first through ninth, in order of when they will hit.

bloop single

A weakly hit fly ball that drops in for a single between an infielder and an outfielder. It's also referred to as a bloop hit or a blooper.

box score

A grid containing a summary of the game statistics, including how each player did.

bullpen

Where the relief pitchers warm up before coming in to pitch. Most stadiums have bullpens beyond the outfield fences, while some have them in foul territory.

bunt

A batting technique used to make a ball difficult to field. The batter holds the bat horizontally instead of swinging. A bunted ball should just bounce off the bat and stay fair so the runners can move up a base.

called up

When a minor league player is moved up or promoted to a major league team to take a spot on its roster. The player may be called up because they have proved themselves in the minor leagues, or because a major leaguer has been placed on the disabled list or sent down to the minor leagues.

catcher

A player who crouches behind home plate to catch any pitches that the batter doesn't hit. If a runner tries to steal a base, the catcher throws the ball to try to get the runner out.

changeup

A slower-than-normal pitch that is thrown using the same arm position as a fastball. It's intended to make the batter swing too soon.

cleanup hitter

The fourth hitter in the batting order. The cleanup hitter is usually the most powerful hitter in the lineup and is expected to "clean up" the bases and drive in runs.

closer

The relief pitcher who comes in to get the final outs.

commentators

The broadcasters or announcers who are at the ballpark describing what is going on in the game for television or radio broadcasts or online streaming. They keep detailed scorecards so they can tell the audience what has happened in the game.

commons

Baseball cards of average players, not superstars. These cards aren't usually valuable to professional collectors, but they still might have value to you if the player is one of your favorites.

contact hitter

A hitter who makes contact with the ball often and doesn't strike out very much.

count

The number of balls and strikes that have been pitched to the hitter. For example, two balls and two strikes would be a "two and two" count. Balls are always listed before strikes.

Cy Young Award

The award given every year to the best pitcher in each league. It's named after the pitcher with the most wins in baseball history.

designated hitter

A player who bats in the lineup instead of the pitcher. The American League uses a designated hitter (DH), but the National League does not—NL pitchers must bat for themselves.

disabled list

When a player is injured the team may put the player on what is called the disabled list, or DL. This means the player cannot play for seven or more days and the team can call someone else up from the minor leagues to put on their roster of active players.

double

A hit that gets the batter safely to second base.

double play

When two base runners are quickly put out after one player hits the ball.

ERA

A pitcher's "earned run average," or how many runs a pitcher is likely to give up in a full nine-inning game. To calculate ERA, multiply the number of earned runs allowed by nine; then divide by the number of innings pitched.

error

When a fielder drops or bobbles a ball or throws it so another fielder can't catch it, resulting in the batter or runner being safe.

extra innings

Additional innings that are played if a game is tied after nine innings. The teams continue to play full innings until someone scores the winning run or runs. The home team always gets the last turn at bat during extra innings.

fastball

A pitch that is thrown as fast as the pitcher can throw it.

foul ball

A ball that is hit by a batter but is not in fair territory. Foul balls count as strike one and strike two, but not as strike three unless you're bunting.

foul line

The lines extending from home plate past first and third base all the way to the outfield fence that separate fair territory from foul territory. A fly ball that lands on the foul line is fair.

foul out

When a ball is hit in the air in foul territory and caught by an opposing player for an out.

foul territory

The part of the playing field that is outside of the foul lines and not part of the actual field of play.

full count

Three balls and two strikes during an at-bat. One more ball means the batter will walk and one more strike is a strikeout.

Gold Glove award

An award for fielding excellence given every year to the best fielder at each position in both the National and American League.

grand slam

A home run that is hit while the bases are loaded (there's a runner on each base), scoring 4 runs, the most runs you can score on 1 hit.

head-to-head league

A type of fantasy league in which your team's stats are compared to one other team's stats on a week-by-week basis.

hit and run

A play where the base runners start running as the pitcher pitches the ball and the batter swings. This play can help avoid a double play and can also get runners to advance more bases on a base hit.

home run

A ball hit in fair territory that goes out of the playing field. A home run scores a run for the batter and any runners on base.

home team

The team that is playing at its own field. The home team bats second in each inning, so they always have the last chance to score runs in the game.

inning

A period of play in which each team has a turn at bat. A professional or college baseball game lasts for nine innings. High school and Little League games are usually shorter—five, six, or seven innings.

infield

The area on the field that is inside the four bases.

infielders

Those who play first base, second base, third base, and shortstop. Infielders play close to the batter and to the bases. They field ground balls and try to throw the batter out. When a ball is hit into the outfield, the infielders receive the ball from the outfielders and try to tag out runners.

intentional walk

When a pitcher walks a batter on purpose. Sometimes this makes it easier to get a double play if there are other runners on second and/or third. Sometimes a batter is walked intentionally because the player is very good and the pitcher doesn't want to give up a home run. An intentional walk is scored as "IW" or "IBB" (intentional base on balls).

left on base

The number of players who were left standing on the bases when the final out was made to end an inning. You may see this in the box score (LOB) or hear broadcasters mention it.

MVP

The abbreviation for "Most Valuable Player." One player in each league wins the MVP award every year, not only for being a great player, but usually for helping their team get to the playoffs. The Baseball Writers' Association of America chooses who wins the MVP award.

no-hitter

When a pitcher allows no hits in a game. It's still a no-hitter if the pitcher walks batters or if batters reach base on fielding errors. In fact, it's possible for a pitcher to pitch a no-hitter but still lose the game.

on deck

The batter scheduled to bat next. Usually there is an on-deck circle on the field where the player stands and takes practice swings.

outfield

The part of the field that is between the infield and the home run fence or wall.

outfielders

The right fielder, left fielder, and center fielder. They play far away from the batter and the bases. Their main job is to catch fly balls and to throw the ball back to the infielders.

pennant

A long, thin, pointed flag—the prize awarded to the teams that win the National League and American League Championship. The two pennant winners play each other in the World Series.

pinch hitter

A hitter who bats in place of someone else.

pinch runner

A player who comes in to run for someone else. This may be a faster runner who can steal a base or score a run more easily than the original base runner.

pitcher

A player who starts all the action on the field by throwing the ball to the batter. Pitchers also field ground balls and help out the infielders.

pitcher's mound

The dirt circle in the middle of the infield diamond where the pitcher stands. It's called a mound because the pitcher stands almost a foot higher than the rest of the infield.

player-manager

A manager of a team who is also a player. Hiring a player to manage the team used to be more common than it is now. The most recent player-manager was Pete Rose, who played for and managed the Reds in 1985 and 1986.

putout

Whenever a fielder performs an action that results in an out. Putouts can happen when a fielder catches a batted ball, steps on a base before a runner touches, or tags a batter who is not on a base. The catcher is credited with an out when catching the ball during a third strike.

rain delay

When a game is stopped because of rain, but they hope to continue and finish it later. The umpires decide when to stop, restart, or call a game (cancel it) because of rain.

rain out

When a game is called off because of rain. If this happens before the fifth inning, the game doesn't count. If it's after the fifth inning it's considered an official game, and whichever team was ahead at the time wins.

relief pitcher

A pitcher who comes in to replace the starting pitcher.

rookie

A first-year player.

roster

The listing of players on the team. Major league rosters include twenty-five players for most of the season.

rotisserie league

A type of fantasy baseball league in which your team's stats are compared to other teams' stats for the whole year.

run

A point scored whenever a player comes all the way around the bases and crosses home plate. The team that scores the most runs wins the game.

runs batted in (RBI)

A statistic that credits a batter for making a play that causes a run to be scored. The most common RBI is a hit that allows one or more players to score a run. Players also receive an RBI for a bases-loaded walk, or when being hit by a pitched ball results in a base runner advancing to score. A run that is scored as an error does not count as an RBI.

sacrifice bunt

When a batter bunts to allow a runner to advance to another base. The hitter is almost always put out, but a sacrifice does not count statistically as a time at bat.

sacrifice fly

When a batter hits a fly ball deep enough to allow a runner on third to tag up and score. A sacrifice fly does not count as a time at bat.

save

When a pitcher comes into a close ballgame and gets the final outs.

scoring position

When a runner is on second or third base, meaning it's easier to score on a hit.

Silver Slugger award

An award for excellence given every year to the best hitter at each position in both the National and American League.

single

A hit that gets the batter safely to first base.

slide

When a runner dives feet first or head first into a base.

southpaw

A left-handed pitcher.

starting pitcher

The pitcher who begins pitching the game for the team.

triple

A hit that gets the batter safely to third base.

triple play

A triple play is a very rare play where one player hits the ball and all three outs are made. Naturally, there has to be no one out and at least two runners on base for a triple play.

umpire

A person who is ruling on the plays in the game. The umpire rules whether a pitch is a strike or a ball; if a ball that is hit is fair or foul; and if a batter or runner is safe or out.

visiting team

The team that comes to play on another team's field. The visiting team always bats first in the inning.

walk-off home run

A home run that is hit in the bottom of the ninth inning or in the bottom of an extra inning that wins the game. Following the home run, the teams walk off the field. The game is over, regardless of how many outs are left, because the opposing team won't have a chance to score.

WHIP

An abbreviation that stands for "Walks plus Hits per Inning Pitched," and means almost the same thing as base runners per inning. Only the very best pitchers' WHIPs are below 1.000. A good WHIP is 1.100 or 1.150.

wild card

One of two teams that qualify for postseason games even though they did not end the season at the top of their division. The winner of each division earns a spot in the playoffs, which means there are three teams at the end of the season who will automatically play for the division pennant. Also, a fourth and fifth team in each league play each other in a one-game "wild card" showdown, with the winners advancing to the quarterfinal series. The wild card survivors have the same chance to win the World Series as any other playoff team; in fact, a wild card team has won the championship seven times since 1994, most recently the Washington Nationals in 2019.

World Series

The annual championship series of MLB, which has been played between the National League (NL) and the American League (AL) each fall since 1903, with two exceptions. In 1904, the New York Giants refused to play the AL champion Boston Americans because they considered the AL to be the "minor" league. And in 1994 the series was canceled due to the players' strike, most recently the Washington Nationals in 2019.

Puzzle Answers

page 15 • Why do hitters...?

Because there are more

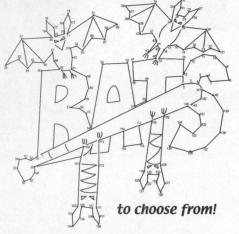

to choose from!

page 24 • Stealing Bases

BALTIMORE ORIOLES

BOSTON RED SOX

NEW YORK METS

BROOKLYN DODGERS

LOS ANGELES ANGELS

ATLANTA BRAVES

page 17 • Curve Ball

F L Y L E B O A R D T O
U P O R R L E R N S J P
G R O M F E S E I R E S
A C U P D A T S C T M D
S S T G I C O S H I R L
T K R U U H H N D S N R
R B O E M O R E P U T O
I O U S R H O T R S G W
H O T T S T O P E S O O
O M D U S H O T M T U B
T D O L R K O T O A T L
R O G D B F E O H D M A

page 29 • Hard Ball

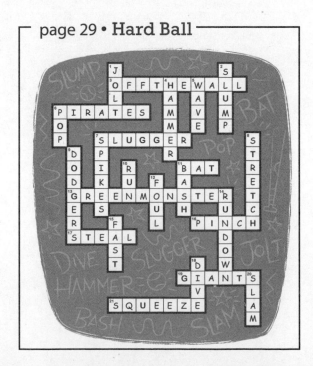

page 41 • Say What?

Y	O	G	I	,	■	I	■	C	A	M	E
H	E	R	E	■	T	O	■	■	H	I	T	,
N	O	T	■	■	T	O	■	R	E	A	D	!

page 55 • Play Ball

1.	Print the word BASEBALL.	**BASEBALL**
2.	Switch the position of the first two letters.	**ABSEBALL**
3.	Move the 5th letter between the 2nd and 3rd letters.	**ABBSEALL**
4.	Switch the positions of the 4th and 8th letters.	**ABBLEALS**
5.	Change the 6th letter to P.	**ABBLEPLS**
6.	Change the last letter to E.	**ABBLEPLE**
7.	Change both B's to P's.	**APPLEPLE**
8.	Change the 7th letter to I.	**APPLEPIE**

page 63 • Switch Hitter

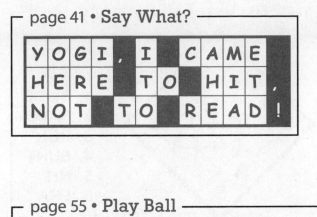

page 66 • Who's Who?

1. The Big Train	_3_	Cy Young
2. Tom Terrific	_5_	Jimmy Foxx
3. Cyclone	_4_	Joe DiMaggio
4. Jotlin' Joe	_7_	Mickey Mantle
5. Double X	_11_	Ozzie Smith
6. Mr. October	_10_	Pete Rose
7. The Mick	_12_	Randy Johnson
8. Say Hey Kid	_6_	Reggie Jackson
9. Stan The Man	_13_	Roger Clemons
10. Charlie Hustle	_9_	Stan Musial
11. Wizard of Oz	_2_	Tom Seaver
12. The Big Unit	_1_	Walter Johnson
13. The Rocket	_8_	Willie Mays

page 70 • Famous Fungo!

__2__ A milk pitcher!

__3__ A catcher's mutt!

__1__ A pancake batter!

page 80 • Baseball Diamond

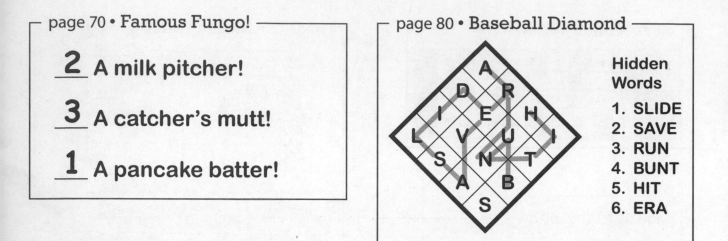

Hidden Words

1. SLIDE
2. SAVE
3. RUN
4. BUNT
5. HIT
6. ERA

page 74 • Hink Pinks

1. The heavier of two batters.
   FATTER BATTER

2. Where you throw a bad referee.
   UMP DUMP

3. Nine baseball players shouting at once.
   TEAM SCREAM

4. The last part of a baseball game when one team has more points.
   WINNING INNING

page 97 • ...Arctic Circle?

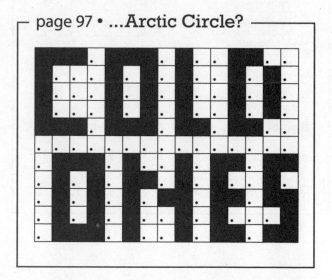

PUZZLE ANSWERS

page 103 • Game Pieces

fly ball

southpaw

home run

bullpen

page 107 • How do you get...?

PLAY BALL!

GAME OVER!

PRACTICE, PRACTICE, PRACTICE!

page 113 • The "Whole World" Series

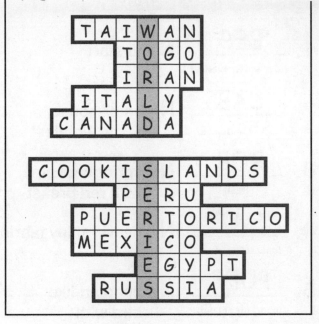

T	A	I	W	A	N
		T	O	G	O
		I	R	A	N
I	T	A	L	Y	
C	A	N	A	D	A

C	O	O	K	I	S	L	A	N	D	S
			P	E	R	U				
P	U	E	R	T	O	R	I	C	O	
M	E	X	I	C	O					
			E	G	Y	P	T			
R	U	S	S	I	A					

page 117 • Name Change

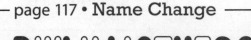

BWLHAICTKESOX

page 119 • Secret Signals

CAREFUL — THIS GUY

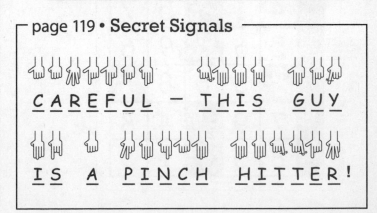

IS A PINCH HITTER!

page 120 • Extra Innings

1. __BEG__ IN = to start
(to plead for money)

2. __CAB__ IN = small house in the woods
(taxi)

3. __ROB__ IN = springtime bird with red breast
(steal)

4. __SAT__ IN = heavy, shiny fabric
(past tense of sit)

5. __PUFF__ IN = penguin-like bird with colorful beak
(short breath out)

page 136 • How come Drew...?

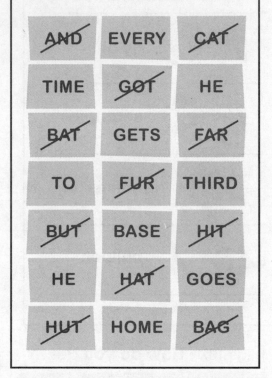

~~AND~~ EVERY ~~CAT~~
TIME ~~GOT~~ HE
~~BAT~~ GETS ~~FAR~~
TO ~~FUR~~ THIRD
~~BUT~~ BASE ~~HIT~~
HE ~~HAT~~ GOES
~~HUT~~ HOME ~~BAG~~

page 132 • Lucky Numbers

page 140 • Dugout

1. UNI_F_ORM
2. GL_ _OVE
3. PLA_Y_OFF
4. _S_LIDE
5. S_W_ING
6. F_A_N
7. BUN_T_
8. CA_T_CHER
9. ST_E_AL
10. R_ _UN

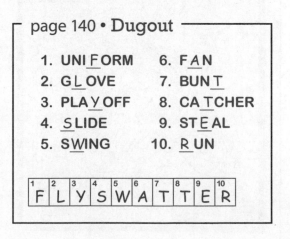

1	2	3	4	5	6	7	8	9	10
F	L	Y	S	W	A	T	T	E	R

PUZZLE ANSWERS

page 143 • The Magic Number

The season has 162 scheduled games.

	won	lost
TEAM A	93	59
TEAM X	89	63

games played so far: **152**

Games TEAM X has won	89
ADD games TEAM X has left	+10
SUBTRACT games TEAM A has won	-93
ADD the number 1	+1
THE MAGIC NUMBER	=7

page 155 • Collectible Words

Possible answers: toll, bite, cell, bill, tile, belt, coil, bell, tell, till, toil, lilt

page 155 • Collectible Cards

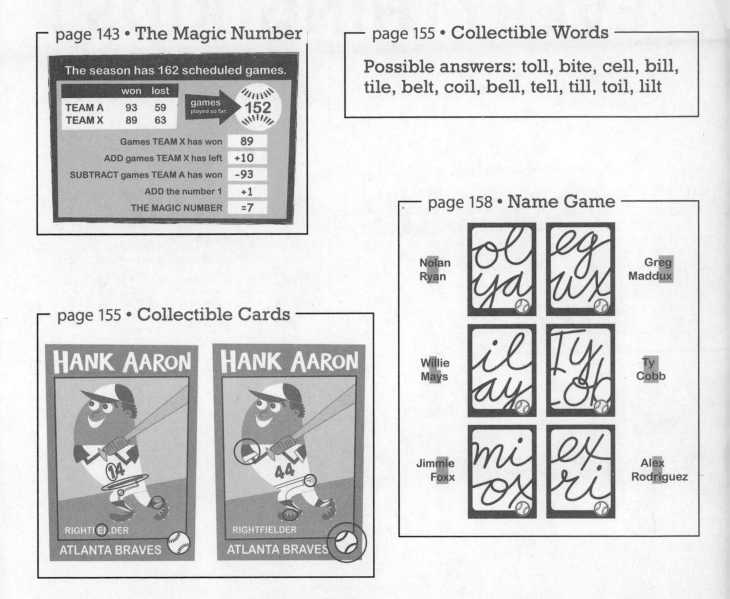

page 158 • Name Game

Nolan Ryan — Greg Maddux
Willie Mays — Ty Cobb
Jimmie Foxx — Alex Rodriguez

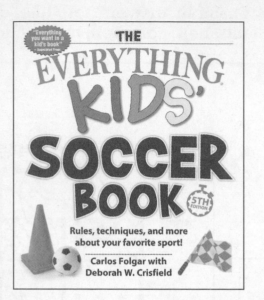
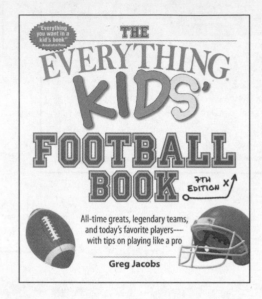
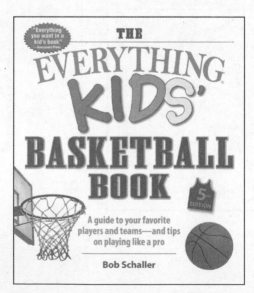